TALENT
UNLEASHED

TALENT

UNLEASHED

*101 Powerful Stories Of Men And
Women Whose Faith, Perseverance,
Determination, Drive, Optimism,
And Ingenuity Triumphed
Over All Obstacles*

Ralph J. Carlson

To order additional copies of this book, contact:
Xlibris Corporation
1-888-795-4274
www.Xlibris.com
Orders@Xlibris.com
17246

CONTENTS

Dedicated to my wonderful wife
Catheryn Jane Kallas Carlson
1932-2000

FOREWORD

Active in community affairs, Mr. Carlson has helped raise thousands of dollars for the March of Dimes, the Muscular Dystrophy Association, Multiple Sclerosis, and numerous other charitable organizations. He personally built three National Exchange Service Clubs.

Mr. Carlson is a veteran of the Korean War (1951-53), and a graduate of the Alexander Hamilton Institute of Business Administration (1965). He was awarded Scouting's Silver Beaver award in 1968, and the "Dick Seddon" award from the Horatio Alger Society in 2000. In 2002, Mr. Carlson was installed in the Utah Broadcasters Association Hall of Fame.

Mr. Carlson resides in Taylorsville, Utah.

Whether your achievements seem humble, such as writing a poem, painting a picture, or repairing a motor, or grandiose, such as the discovery of a cure for Parkinson's or Alzheimer's or writing the next best-selling novel, only you know what you might accomplish.

CHAPTER 1

Perseverance/Survivor

Pedro De Serrano

It was 1540. In the middle of the Pacific Ocean, a ship sank suddenly in the night without warning. The only man not to perish was Pedro De Serrano. As he went overboard, all he had were the clothes he was wearing and a knife he had tucked into his belt. As he swam onto the shore of an unnamed island, he saw no sign of life, only a vast expanse of sand. Serrano had landed on an island where there were no trees, water, or grass.

The next morning, Serrano surveyed the situation and went to work. He put aside his worries and looked for ways to survive. His first task was to explore the island. Along the beach he found cockles, shrimp, and other small sea creatures that had washed ashore. These he ate raw. As he continued, Serrano also found some turtles near the shore. He successfully hunted several with his knife and ate their meat. He cleaned out the shells and let them dry. He later used the smaller shells to scoop rainwater from puddles, which in turn were poured into the larger shells for storage. Some of the shells, used as reserve tanks, held up to 12 gallons of precious fresh water.

Possessing nothing with which to start a fire, Serrano scoured the island looking for two pebbles that would adequately serve as flints against his knife. Unable to find any on land, he took to the ocean. After multiple dives, Serrano finally found some suitable stones that he honed to the right shape for creating sparks. He built a fire using seaweed, driftwood, and fibers from his shirt. Once lit, he kept the fire going, even using turtle shells to protect it from rough weather.

It took seven years before sailors saw the smoke from Serrano's fire and rescued him.

Serrano found a way to survive despite great odds against him. He didn't panic or surrender to his plight, but instead thought his way to survival.

CHAPTER 2

Determination/Salesman

Ron Popeil

*V*eg-O-Matic king Ron Popeil founded the very successful *Ronco, Inc. and then lost it all when his bank pulled his credit line. His "rags to riches" story is unique because he had to do it twice.*

At age 16, Popeil started selling his father's kitchen gadgets, ranging from the Popeil Donut Maker to the Slice-A-Way cutting board. Armed with nothing more than a microphone and his inventory, he was pitching products up to 10 hours a day on Chicago's Maxwell Street. Working from 5 A.M. to dusk, Popeil grabbed the attention of passersby with his gift of gab and his relentless enthusiasm.

By age 19 he convinced the manager of a Chicago Woolworth store to sell on the floor as an independent agent. So confident was Popeil of his salesmanship that he agreed to a deal where the store would pay him nothing and he would give Woolworth 20 percent of his revenue. He wound up working 12-hour shifts and netting $1,000 per week, a small fortune in the mid-1950s.

By the late 1950s, he was advertising Popeil products on television. In 1964, he started Ronco, Inc., selling his father's products and some of his own inventions. Popeil took the company public in 1969 at the age of 34. His company thrived through the 1970s, and his empire grew.

In the mid-1980s, though, Popeil faced the challenge of his life. A large Illinois bank had to be bailed out by the federal government due to bad loans. The ripple effect of the bailout extended to Popeil's lender, First National Bank. In 1983, Ronco's loan was called—a $15 million line of revolving credit. A year later the bank took over Ronco's receivables. Unable to spend money on advertising, Ronco filed for reorganization under Chapter 11, and in 1987 the company was liquidated under Chapter 7.

Despite the bankruptcy setback, Popeil remained confident in his sales ability and products. He had been smart enough not to guarantee any loans personally and was thereby able to hold onto his own assets. After the bankruptcy, Popeil was able to buy back Ronco's inventory for $2 million at auction. By early 1989, he had made back his $2 million and then some.

In 1991, he returned to television with his half-hour "Incredible Inventions" infomercials. Within a year and a half he had generated over $20 million in revenue. Currently, Popeil is still doing infomercials and has branched out to the television shopping network giant, QVC Inc. His sales on QVC bring in about $1 million during each 24-hour series.

His advice is to stay focused regardless of the circumstances. His philosophy is to keep moving forward no matter what a person encounters.

CHAPTER 3

Loyalty/Military

Jeremiah Denton Jr.

The North Vietnamese beat Jeremiah Denton Jr. viciously. They tortured him, confined him to tiny cells, and starved him. But they couldn't make him betray his country.

His loyalty was most evident in May 1966, when Denton was in his 10th month as a prisoner of war in Hanoi. The North Vietnamese were trying to force Denton and other POWs to condemn the U.S. for its Vietnam War policy. The North Vietnamese used a Japanese journalist to do the questioning, perhaps as an attempt to give the "interviews" a more credible appearance. One by one, the POWs denounced the U.S. government.

When Denton was questioned he said to the North Vietnamese that he didn't know what was happening in Vietnam, but he said whatever the position of his government was, he would support it as long as he lived. He was aware that he was risking further torture by refusing to waver from his convictions.

In his interview, Denton was able to give the first clear sign to the American people that he and the other POWs were being tortured by their captors. Blinding floodlights that were used during filming caused him to blink, so he cleverly employed the Morse code by blinking slowly for dashes and quickly for dots. He repeatedly spelled out "torture" with his blinks, hoping U.S. Intelligence officials would heed his message. They did.

On July 18, 1965, Denton was a fighter pilot leading a group of 28 aircrafts on an attack of North Vietnamese targets. His plane was shot down, and after parachuting to the ground he was captured and taken to Hanoi. For seven years and seven months, Denton paid for being faithful to his country. He was beaten. He spent days shackled and in total darkness. He endured lengthy solitary confinement on a 47-inch-by-47-inch concrete square. His bed was a stone slab, accompanied only by rats and huge insects.

At times, Denton wanted to die but willed himself to survive. He relied on three key elements to keep himself going. One was prayer and surrendering himself to God. Another was reciting inspirational works from America's Founding Fathers. A third was staying in regular contact with his fellow POWs, a tall order since the prisoners were forbidden to talk. Denton invented a covert communications system that involved coughs, sniffs, throat clearing, hacks, spits, and wall tapping.

Denton was honored for his bravery upon returning to the U.S. in 1973. He received multiple decorations, including the Navy Cross, the branch's most prestigious medal. He later served as a U.S. senator from Alabama from 1981 to 1987.

Denton survived his ordeal by taking one minute at a time.

CHAPTER 4

Persistence/Cell Phones

Martin Cooper

Martin Cooper had a vision: a phone that could be carried around and powered by a battery. Many of his fellow engineers scoffed at his notion. But Cooper had a secret weapon to make his vision a reality—persistence.

Vowing to keep working until he'd completed the job, Cooper spent more than half his career as a researcher with Motorola Inc. working on the project. It took 15 years and cost $90 million for Motorola to take the cellular phone concept to market.

Cooper faced a lot of skeptics, but he kept his focus and sold people on the idea. Today he is known as the father of the cellular telephone.

The handheld cell phone might seem like a no-brainer now, but it wasn't in 1973 when Cooper tested the first prototype on a New York City street corner. Back then, AT&T was focused on selling car telephones and pooh-poohed the portable cell phone. That is why the first call Cooper made, using the two-pound prototype, was to an acquaintance at AT&T's Bell Laboratories.

Cooper and Motorola worked for 10 years to bring the cell phone to the commercial market after the first prototype. "There were a lot of naysayers over the years," Cooper said. "People would say, 'Why are you spending all of this money? Are you sure this cellular thing will turn out to be something?' Before cellular was started, there were only about 50,000 car telephones in the United States. And here we were starting a business that required millions of subscribers to be successful."

To convince the skeptics, Cooper relied on his ability to explain complex technologies in simple terms and used his ability to match technology ideas with business markets. He even learned to appreciate skeptics. Cooper's philosophy was that he appreciated skeptics questioning new ideas, that they provided a sorting out because for every hundred ideas, only a few are successful. The skeptics do you a big favor.

Today one would be hard-pressed to find a car phone.

Persistence is often needed for dreams to come to fruition.

CHAPTER 5

Faith/Freedom

William Bradford

William Bradford dreamed of freedom: the freedom to worship as he wished, without fear of persecution. To do this he would have to risk death. In September 1860, he and 101 others boarded the *Mayflower*. The passengers knew of the vast, rough ocean that lay ahead and of the unknown wilderness that they would find on the other side.

Bradford was completely focused on his goal. He said to his fellow passengers, who were unsure if they could face such perils, that it takes risk to achieve something worth having. Sixty-five days later, Bradford and his fellow Puritans anchored in Plymouth Harbor off what would become the state of Massachusetts.

In April 1861, Bradford was elected governor of Plymouth Colony at the age of 31. He would be re-elected 30 times in the next 35 years, serving until his death in 1657. He helped write the Mayflower Compact, a primer for self-government and just and equal laws.

Bradford was born in Yorkshire, England, and was orphaned by age 7. At 12, in spite of his relative's warnings, he joined a Separatist church, the most extreme part of the Puritan movement, which aimed to reform the Church of England. Many Separatists perished for their beliefs, but Bradford wanted to encourage change rather than to fear it.

Figuring he had to be well informed to effect change, Bradford delved into study. He sought out books and mentors to expand his knowledge. He became fluent in Dutch, French, Latin, Greek, and Hebrew. He also mastered history, theology, and philosophy.

In 1608, Bradford and 470 others fled England to go to Holland and search for religious freedom. Although safer, the exiles still needed a place where they could build their ideal community from the ground up. Bradford saw America as the answer.

Only 50 of the original settlers made it through the first winter in the New World. For several years there were food shortages. Bradford noticed the communal crops weren't producing a large harvest enough to feed everyone. He devised a plan to assign every family a parcel of land to cultivate as they wished. With this change came a greater sense of personal responsibility and with it associated industriousness. Food shortages were overcome.

Bradford was so admired because he encouraged people to voice their opinions, and he listened to their concerns. It has been said that without his determination, fairness, generosity, and well-tempered spirit the colony would not have survived.

"All great and honorable actions are accompanied with great difficulties," Bradford said.

CHAPTER 6

Determination/Cameras

Oskar Barnack

Oskar Barnack was born near Berlin, Germany, in 1879. As a child he suffered from severe asthma attacks, and many thought he should lead the life of an invalid. But Barnack refused to let the ailment rule his life.

Instead, Barnack overcame his illness to invent the 35 mm camera called the Leica. It was the first precision miniature camera to become commercially available and change the photography industry.

As a youth, Barnack was persuaded by his father to apprentice with an instrument maker. When he reached journeymen status, Barnack went from job to job searching for a master he could learn from. He found his calling when hired by the Carl Zeiss works in Jena, Germany, to learn optics. Barnack diligently learned all he could about telescopes, microscopes, and lenses. During his time away from work he eagerly pursued photography. However, Barnack's asthma limited him. The large-format camera and its accessories proved to be heavy and cumbersome, especially for one with breathing limitations. He dreamed of a handy, lightweight camera and resolved to come up with one.

In 1911, Barnack landed a job as the head of design and development at Ernst Leitz optical works in Wetzlar, Germany, and by 1912, he was working on the development of the cine camera. The fine grain of the motion picture film inspired him to revisit his original experiments involving the creation of a small camera. Barnack believed that the cine film was the key to the smaller camera. Cine film was readily available worldwide, and its perforations were ideal for positioning and transporting the film in the camera. By taking an existing camera body and reworking it to accommodate precision workings, Barnack was able to combine two cine frames into a single frame.

Barnack's hard work paid off in 1913. He had made a small camera that used 35 mm motion picture negative film instead of heavy glass plates. This would later become the classic 35 mm camera.

The First World War slowed Barnack's development on his camera. Leitz was diverted to produce binoculars and rangefinders for the German war effort. Barnack used what little free time he had to improve the design and function of the miniature camera, and by 1924, the improved camera was almost ready to go into production. Many prominent experts discouraged Barnack from making the small, unconventional camera. They felt that because of its high price, there would be no market for it. Barnack ignored the critics and convinced Leitz to put the camera into production. Producing the camera did indeed prove expensive, but Barnack insisted that only the best materials be used and that no shortcuts were to be taken.

The 35 mm Leica camera was introduced to the public at the Leipzig Spring Fair in 1925. By 1938, production grew to 38,000 Leicas. Barnack continued to make improvements on his camera until his death in 1936.

Rather than allow his medical condition to become his crutch, Barnack instead chose to use it as his motivation.

CHAPTER 7

Innovation/Pianos

Henry Steinway

Heinrich Engelhard Steinweg (1797-1871) was born the youngest of twelve children in Wolshagen, Germany. By age 15, in the year 1812, he was the only one remaining of his family. Penniless, the young Steinweg supported himself doing odd jobs until he was old enough to join the German Army in 1815, serving until he was 22.

During times of peace Steinweg used his time in the army to learn woodworking and cabinetmaking. He discovered he loved working with his hands and especially making musical instruments. After his discharge, Steinweg found a job at an organ-building firm in Goslar, Germany. But Steinweg was too impatient to work the seven—or eight-year apprenticeship and moved to Seesen, Germany, after only a year's training. There he set up shop as a cabinetmaker and pipe organ repairman. His free time was spent learning more about an instrument that fascinated him, the piano.

Once he had learned how to build them, Steinweg experimented with different ways to improve the piano. He tried different woods and perfected the cut of the keyboard and the regulating of the action and the strings. He developed a stronger piano by introducing a cast-iron frame that made it possible to put greater tension on the strings. This structure resulted in a heartier piano with a bigger sound and more dynamic range.

In 1825, Steinweg married, and he played the organ at his own wedding. His piano was tremendously successful and his six sons went to work with him as soon as they were old enough to hold a tuning fork. Steinweg knew that it was important to teach his sons the instrument construction process in order to preserve his methods. His first grand piano was completed in 1836 and was later purchased by the Duke of Brunswick for 300 marks.

With the help of his sons, Steinweg was able to produce as many as ten pianos a year. However, in 1830, the German economy was suffering a severe recession and his business lagged. Steinweg stuck with his craft, but by 1848, he began looking for new opportunities. At age 53, he uprooted his family and business and moved to the U.S., arriving in New York City on June 29, 1850.

Once in New York, Steinweg found work in a piano factory. His sons worked in cabinetry shops in town. After hours they made pianos at home and sold them on the side. In less than a year in the U.S., Steinweg was able to establish his own business, Steinway & Sons. Due to discrimination against Germans in New York at the time, he had changed his name to Henry Engelhard Steinway, feeling that in order to be successful he must Americanize his name.

The company prospered, and by 1860, his business necessitated a larger location. Steinway announced the grand opening of the new factory in 1864. To entice curious onlookers to become customers, he made the showroom as beautiful as possible. A local newspaper raved that the salesroom was probably the finest in the world.

More family sorrows were soon to befall Steinway. Son Henry Jr. died of tuberculosis and son Charles died of typhoid fever, both in March of 1865. Steinway's grief was compounded by labor unrest at the factory, which culminated in a strike in May. He was left to manage the factory and showroom with his two youngest and least-experienced sons.

Rather than giving up, Steinway persuaded his son Christian, who had remained in Germany, to come to New York. With this additional support, Steinway was able to focus on increasing his business. In addition to improving his products, Steinway designed an upright piano designed to fit in smaller homes. The upright piano became enormously popular and Steinway received 11 patents for his innovations to it.

Steinway's innovations and his refusal to give up produced the standard by which all pianos are measured today.

CHAPTER 8

Attitude/Kevlar

Stephanie Kwolek

B ecause Stephanie Kwolek stood her ground, thousands of
people are alive today who could otherwise have died.

It was 1964, and Kwolek had been assigned by Dupont Co. to
help develop the next generation of high-performance polymer
fibers. She'd come up with a cloudy chemical solution for which
she had high hopes, but a colleague told her that a cloudy solution
couldn't possibly generate any polymer fibers. A cloudy solution
usually indicated the presence of solid particles, and because of
these particles, the tiny tubes of the spinnerets would clog and no
fibers would be formed.

Rather than scrap her solution in the face of what seemed to
be a scientific certainty, Kwolek stood fast. She had done her
homework, having already noted that the solution's cloudiness
appeared iridescent when stirred. That wasn't characteristic of
particles, which are typically gray or white.

Wanting to be absolutely sure that her solution was viable,
Kwolek went back to the lab. She retested the solution by putting
it through a fine filter. She saw the solution was still cloudy even
after being filtered, indicating for certain that the solution did not
contain any particles. Still not knowing what the solution was,
Kwolek kept performing tests on it until it was determined that

she had invented the world's first synthetic liquid crystals. The cloudy appearance was due to light diffraction off the crystals.

Once the solution was put through the spinneret, the liquid crystals formed fibers that were strong and stiff. When interwoven, they became Kevlar. Five times stronger than steel, ounce for ounce, Kevlar is mainly used for bullet-resistant body armor. According to the Kevlar Survivors Club, more than 2,000 lives have been saved by Kevlar armor. Kevlar has other uses as well, including the mooring lines used by over half of the U.S. Navy's ships. It is also used in fiber-optic cables, lifting slings, and as protective wear in cutting occupations.

Kwolek, born in 1923, was just 10 when her father died. Her mother was forced to work odd jobs in the Depression-era economy in order to keep the family together. From her mother Kwolek learned to be strong-willed and hardworking. She also absorbed her mother's "can-do" attitude. These characteristics helped her earn a degree in Chemistry and enter the workforce that was then considered to be a man's job. Her positive attitude and tight focus earned her the respect of her colleagues, and she was rewarded with increasingly challenging projects. Kwolek holds 17 patents and has received her industry's most prestigious awards.

Kwolek knew that she would eventually succeed, but a person has to pay the price and do the work that's needed.

CHAPTER 9

Resolve/Reformer

Dorothea Dix

Dorothea Dix hid her shock and anger as she looked into a jail cell in March 1841 at two shivering, barely clothed women. The women were mentally ill and had no family to care for them. Officials in East Cambridge, Massachusetts, had tossed them into an empty prison cell without bedding, furniture, or even a bucket for waste. Though the temperature at times dropped below zero, the jailers refused to give the women blankets or clothing. At that time, many people believed that the insane were immune to cold and pain.

Dix knew that in order to help these women she would have to persuade the local officials to order the jailers to change their ways. This task would be difficult as Dix had no political allies and she didn't come from an influential family. She formulated a plan and was able to convince two Massachusetts leaders, educator Samuel Gridley Howe and legislator Charles Sumner, to inspect the prison themselves. Once they'd seen the conditions, they rallied for her cause. She also wrote letters to as many influential people as possible to tell of the women's plight. Her efforts paid off, as the court ordered the jailers to improve the women's living conditions.

Because of the public awareness Dix had generated, she learned that across the country, mentally ill people were subjected to even worse treatment than at the East Cambridge jail. Some were sold as servants and confined in cages, pens, and underground pits. Others were tied to chairs, doused with ice-cold water, leeched, beaten, and starved. Because she believed that the mentally ill should be treated humanely, Dix was determined to try to persuade the nation's legislators to change laws and to fund new institutions. Once again, she devised a plan.

In 1841 and 1842, Dix traveled more than 8,000 miles by carriage, steamboat, barge, lumber wagon, horse and stagecoach to visit every jail, asylum, and hospital in her state. Upon each inspection, she chronicled the heinous conditions and, at the end of her travels, submitted the document to the Massachusetts Legislature. Her work convinced the lawmakers to improve conditions for the state's mentally ill and to increase funding for public hospitals.

Having succeeded on the state level, Dix set her sights on the entire nation. By the end of 1849, she had traveled more than 60,000 miles by stagecoach and had visited 400 American cities: all the time observing the conditions of the mentally ill. Dix stressed that she was not condemning officials but trying to reform a cruel, outdated system. But when she found outrageous practices at facilities, she did not hesitate to report the administrators who were responsible.

Dix again expanded her campaign, this time to Europe. She was granted an audience with Pope Pius IX, who, after hearing her reports, promised to inspect Roman asylums personally.

Before becoming a reformer, Dix was a schoolteacher. She wrote seven books by age 30, her most famous being a four-volume children's encyclopedia which covered 300 topics. Over the next 45 years it would go through 60 printings. She died in 1887 in Trenton, New Jersey.

Dorothea Dix improved the lives of countless people because she decided that it was better to take action than to passively complain.

CHAPTER 10

Drive/Electronics

Simon Ramo

Simon Ramo knew from boyhood that he never wanted to settle for second best. Growing up in Salt Lake City, Ramo was considered to be something of a prodigy at the violin. At age 12, he heard virtuoso Jascha Heifetz play and realized he would never achieve the level of skill Heifetz demonstrated that evening. It was then that Ramo decided he couldn't pursue music as a career, so he turned to his other passion—science.

It was a good decision. Ramo went on to co-found TRW Inc. He led the team that developed America's intercontinental ballistic missile (ICBM) and helped lead the research that forged America's lead in space technology.

Born in 1913, Ramo earned a B.S. in electrical engineering from the University of Utah by age 20. By 23, he had earned doctorate degrees in both physics and electrical engineering from the California Institute of Technology. After college, Ramo worked in the research department of General Electric. He constantly tried new ideas and developed the company's electron microscope. By the end of World War II, he held 25 patents in electronics.

Ramo felt the need to branch out even more instead of working on someone else's ideas. When he learned that Hughes Aircraft wanted to expand its research efforts after the war, he eagerly joined.

Ramo focused on pioneering work for the U.S. Air Force in guided missile systems. In 1953, Ramo and Dean Woolridge left Hughes and formed the Ramo-Woolridge Corp. to pursue electronics. Three years later, auto parts maker Thompson Products was brought on board to form the company TRW.

The young company was assigned by the government to spearhead a program to catch up with the Soviet's ICBM advances. Initially, Ramo didn't want the assignment because it meant placing all of the company's resources into one basket, but his patriotism eventually won out. Once he'd made the decision, Ramo threw all of his energy and resources behind the effort. His efforts allowed the U.S. to overcome the early Soviet advantages in the ICBM race. Ramo later founded the Space Technology Laboratory (STL), which became the center of research for America's space effort. Much of the groundwork for the early satellite launches took place at the STL.

Ramo attributes his ability to anticipate the future as being in the right place at the right time. If you're reasonably good, you'll be able to see the next step.

CHAPTER 11

Ingenuity/Train Engines

Mathias Baldwin

The depression of 1837 hit Mathias Baldwin hard. One of Philadelphia's top industrial magnates, the locomotive maker had just completed a $200,000 plant, expecting engine orders to escalate. Instead, they plummeted as the economy collapsed. Many of Baldwin's customers stopped paying him, leaving nothing with which to pay his creditors. But Baldwin had a strong sense of duty and refused to request leniency from creditors. He insisted on paying every penny he owed. He took drastic measures—laying off employees and accepting a new partner. Still, he broke even by 1842.

Baldwin had long been a tinkerer. Born in Elizabethtown, New Jersey, in 1795, he worked as an apprentice at a jewelry firm. After completing the apprenticeship, Baldwin started making jewelry for Fletcher & Gardener. He learned metalworking from the seasoned jewelers. In 1824, Baldwin figured he could use his skills with larger pieces of metal. He opened a shop with another Philadelphia mechanic. When they needed a larger power supply they looked at steam engines. Baldwin found that there weren't any stationary ones available, so in 1829 he built his own.

Baldwin used a novel and ingenious plan to build his stationary steam engine. It occupied the least possible space, yet created more than enough power. Soon, other people wanted Baldwin to build them steam engines. In 1831, he was hired by a local railroad to build a locomotive. Baldwin took the best features from a contemporary English engine and incorporated his improvements. Christened Old Ironsides, the newfangled locomotive hit 28 mph on its test run—an impressive speed for 1832.

Baldwin Locomotive Works was launched. But Old Ironsides had problems and ran aground on its first passenger trip.

Baldwin tried correcting everything but became so frustrated that he proclaimed: "This is our last locomotive." But Baldwin was too driven to give up so hastily. He weighed his options and decided to try again. He made improvements in the locomotive's ability to handle tight curves and improved adhesion to the rails. He came up a flexible beam that transmitted power to three axles. Baldwin also invented the half-crank, which allowed for a larger boiler to create more power. Because of these and other innovations, Baldwin's locomotives became the best in the industry. Baldwin Locomotive Works became the world's largest locomotive maker in the nineteenth and early twentieth centuries.

Baldwin's business philosophy was simple but kept his company at the top: *Make sure you put your customers' needs first, buy the highest-quality materials available, and hire the best people you can find.*

CHAPTER 12

Determination/Confidence

Helen Keller

Helen Keller wasn't just blind; she was also completely deaf. So when she announced her intention to attend a regular college, her family and friends were aghast. But Keller knew what she wanted, and she was determined to get it.

Keller was born a normal, healthy infant in 1880. At age 19 months, a high fever robbed her of both sight and hearing. Unable to communicate, she threw violent rages—kicking, biting, and pinching family members and breaking things. Some relatives urged her parents to commit her to an insane asylum. Instead, they searched for her a tutor. When Helen was 7 they hired Annie Sullivan, a partly blind 24-year-old teacher.

Sullivan decided to try a touch-based version of American Sign Language to teach Keller how to communicate. It was the key Keller needed to unlock the outside world. By spelling out words in the palm of Keller's hand, Sullivan taught her how to identify objects, spell, read, and—best of all—communicate with others. Keller later called Sullivan's arrival "the most important day of my life."

With Sullivan at her side, Keller enrolled in the Perkins School for the Blind in Boston. An eager learner, Keller later went for two years to the Cambridge School, a college-preparatory academy for girls. During Keller's first weeks at Cambridge, it looked as though she might have to drop out. Few of the textbooks were available in Braille, and she couldn't take notes in class because Sullivan had to spell out the lectures in her outstretched hand. In an effort to keep up, Keller would rush to her room each day and type whatever she could remember on her Braille typewriter. Keller faced further challenges as Braille had yet to be standardized, forcing her to learn five different versions.

Keller's dedication helped her pass all her college-preparatory courses at Cambridge, including French, German, Latin, and Greek. She then shocked her acquaintances by announcing that she would apply to Radcliffe College. The board of Radcliffe tried to discourage her, but Keller clung to her dream of a college education with fierce determination. She prepared for and took the college's nine-hour entrance exams. Not only did Keller pass, but her performance was rated "excellent." Four years later, in 1904, Keller graduated cum laude.

After college, Keller shifted her focus to humanitarian concerns. Her book *Out of the Dark*, in 1920 explored the social problems of the time—poor housing, joblessness, war, hunger, and crime. She also penned articles on women's suffrage, politics, and world economics. Sadly, the American public rejected these writings. People only seemed interested in Keller's life as a disabled person. She decided to turn her attention to helping others who were blind.

Keller strove to change the public's perception of blind people. She asked that people not treat the blind as helpless objects of pity. She believed that the blind should be given the opportunity to support themselves through training and jobs. Keller also encouraged other disabled people to rise above their limitations.

One of Keller's greatest achievements was the standardization of Braille. Her relentless appearances before Congress spurred legislators to create a national system of libraries for the blind under the Library of Congress. In 1921, Keller accepted a fund-raising position with the American Foundation for the Blind. During her 123-city tour she raised more that $1 million for the AFB.

> *"You must face your deficiencies and acknowledge them, but do not let them master you. When we do the best we can, we never know what miracle is wrought in our life, or in the life of another."*—Helen Keller

CHAPTER 13

Optimism/Air-Conditioning

Willis Carrier

For centuries, people had tried different approaches to cooling homes, public areas, and workspaces. And for centuries, their solutions had proved to be temporary at best. The practice of pumping air over snow or ice was both inefficient and messy. But Willis Carrier, the father of air-conditioning, was certain there had to be a clean and effective way to cool air.

In 1902, the Sackett-Wilhelms Lithography and Publishing Co. in New York asked Carrier, a mechanical engineer, to figure out how to chill and dry the muggy summer air. Besides the unpleasantness to the employees, the hot, humid air made the ink runny and the paper limp. Carrier didn't jump into action right away. Instead he put on his thinking cap. He determined the optimum humidity for printing by poring over weather information. He studied chemicals that would take water out of the atmosphere. He learned how air moved as it went around corners and metal coils. Once his research was done, Carrier built his machine.

A few months later, Carrier installed his first air conditioner at Sackett-Wilhelms. It sucked air over coils holding chilled calcium chloride brine. When the air was blown back into the room, it was dry, clean, and chilled. His clients were thrilled. Carrier's air conditioner had the cooling power of melting 54 tons of ice every day.

Despite the success of his first air conditioner, Carrier pushed himself to do even better. He made it a point to keep his mind at work even when he wasn't behind a desk. One foggy night, while waiting for a train in Pittsburgh, Carrier was looking out into the fog. Suddenly, Carrier realized that if he could wash the air with a fog-like mist, he'd be able to cool it without the use of calcium chloride. This would reduce both the cost and the maintenance of the air conditioner. By 1906, he patented a new version of his air conditioner that did just that.

Industries around the U.S. scrambled to improve working conditions with Carrier's new air conditioner. Business was booming, but Carrier continued to improve his product and his customer base. Carrier Corp., started in 1915, is currently the world's largest supplier of climate-control equipment, with worldwide sales exceeding $5 billion.

Carrier felt that he could succeed at anything by trying hard. He displayed enthusiasm whether at play, work or studying.

CHAPTER 14

Daring/Seaman

John Paul Jones

John Paul Jones is often called the father of the U.S. Navy. He turned the tide of the Rrvolutionary by using tough guerilla tactics.

In the 1770s, American ships focused on capturing British merchant ships off the coast of New England. But Jones figured out that he had to take the fight to the British if the war was to be won. Commanding the ship *Providence*, Jones was able to destroy eight ships and capture eight others in one outing. The English began referring to him as "the pirate John Paul."

In 1777, Jones was assigned to sail to France in the ship *Ranger* to retrieve a newly built heavy frigate. On the way, Jones captured two merchant ships as prizes. Upon reaching France, he found that the frigate *L'Indien* was no longer available. The U.S. had given it to France as a gift. Undeterred, Jones sailed to the Irish coast, sinking, burning, and capturing English ships along the way. The Ranger even raided the English coastline. News of the brazen attacks swept through England, with the psychological impact far outweighing the actual damage done.

Jones and the U.S. Ambassador to France, Benjamin Franklin, decided to keep up the pressure with more raids on England. As captain of the *Bon Homme Richard*, Jones encountered the larger, 44-gun English ship HMS *Serapis* and engaged it in battle on the coast of England. After three hours of furious fighting, Jones had lost half of his men, and his ship had started to sink after being rammed by the *Serapis*. Jones refused to give up the fight. He lashed the *Bon Homme Richard* to the *Serapis*, and his remaining crew engaged the English in hand-to-hand combat. When all looked to be lost, Jones decided to motivate his men by example. When Capt. Richard Person of the *Serapis* asked for his surrender, John replied, "I have not yet begun to fight!" Shaken by the fury of the attack, Person later surrendered the *Serapis*.

After the revolutionary war officially ended in 1784, Jones returned to France. King Louis XVI bestowed him with the title of chevalier, an equivalent of knighthood in England. During his final visit to the U.S. in 1787, Congress awarded his with a gold medal, the only one given to an officer of the Continental Navy. Jones later accepted an invitation from Catherine the Great to head Russia's naval effort against Turkey.

While living abroad after the war, Jones wrote Thomas Jefferson to reassure him he could *"never renounce the glorious title of a citizen of the United States."*

CHAPTER 15

Innovation/Creator

Walt Disney

It was 1928, and the 26-year-old cartoon animator was taking the train back to California after a disastrous trip to New York. His sly distributor had just taken over the rights to Disney's first big-time character, Oswald the Lucky Rabbit, hiring away Disney's best animators in the process.

Even though his studio was in debt and he had lost his staff, Disney wouldn't admit defeat. He vowed to start over with what he still possessed—his talent. As the train sped through the Midwest, Disney started doodling. It wasn't long before Disney thought that two doodles looked like a mouse. He was at first inclined to call his new character "Mortimer," but his wife suggested "Mickey." Disney had just created Mickey Mouse, who would become the most popular cartoon figure in the world, at a time when his future looked its dimmest.

Disney's persistence would lead him to ever-greater achievement in cartoon animation. During his career of more than 40 years, Disney's studio set the standard for animated and family films, winning 48 Academy Awards in the process.

As a boy, Disney drew whenever he had a chance. He drew animals on toilet paper and filled the margins of his notebooks with cartoon characters. In France, while working for the Red Cross

Ambulance Corps in World War I, Disney practiced his skills by decorating his friends' helmets and jackets. By the time he returned to the U.S. in 1919, the 18-year-old Disney opened his first commercial art business in Kansas City, Missouri. The studio closed within a year, mainly due to Disney's lack of business experience, but it set him on his career path.

After working as an animator for three years, Disney opened Disney Bros. Studio with his brother Roy. As soon as profits came in, Disney spent them on an innovation. First he added sound to his cartoons, then he added color. *Steamboat Willie*, a cartoon featuring Mickey Mouse, was the first to use sound. *Flowers and Trees*, released in 1932, was the first animated feature to use technicolor. His early success with Mickey Mouse was sustained by his creation of Donald Duck in 1934.

Disney's next idea to produce a full-length, animated feature was met with opposition. His distributors worried about changing what was already working, and his family worried about gambling away profits. Disney ignored them all, spending an astronomical $2 million in the depths of the Depression, and he released *Snow White and the Seven Dwarfs* in 1937. It was an instant hit, and a new genre of animation was created. During the next five years, Disney completed more full-length animated classics such as *Pinocchio*, *Fantasia*, *Dumbo* and *Bambi*.

Disney had a vision of creating an amusement park where all his ideas and characters could come to life. In the 1950s, though, amusement park owners told him he was out of his mind. Once again, Disney believed in himself and his ideas in spite of his critics. He borrowed $100,000 against his life insurance policy, sold his vacation home in Palm Springs, and started raising additional capital through his *Disneyland* television series. In 1955, he founded the Disneyland theme park. Disney's empire has been growing ever since.

Disney's success has been attributed to the fact that he never tried to make money. Disney believed that if he made a project as good as he possibly could, people would like it and profits would eventually follow. "I've only thought of money in one way," Disney said, "and that is to do something with. I plow back everything I make into the company. I look at it this way: If I can't use the money now, if I can't have fun with it, I'm not going to be able to take it with me."

"Disney had only one rule," said an animator. *"Whatever we did had to be better than anybody else could do it."*

CHAPTER 16

Entrepreneur/Hats

John Batterson Stetson

John Batterson Stetson hated the patter of raindrops on his head. He knew the rain would only worsen his hacking cough and tuberculosis. One of 12 children, Stetson grew up as a frail, sickly child diagnosed with "lung trouble" and given only a few months to live. On doctor's advice, he moved to the West from Philadelphia around 1859, seeking dry, hot weather to heal his lungs.

But Stetson found the Western climate to be anything but dry. The brick factory he ran in St. Joseph, Missouri, was swept away by the Missouri River. After being rejected by the army during the Civil War, Stetson headed to Colorado to pan for gold. He found the rugged life made him sicker.

When trapped in the mountains and threatened by sudden rainstorms and howling winds, ordinary clothing didn't keep him dry. Stetson knew he had to act fast to protect himself or risk dying. He observed beavers in a nearby stream and saw how their pelts repelled water and kept them warm. After shooting some, Stetson boiled and kneaded the fur and pounded it into felt, a skill he had learned from his hat-making father as a child. From this he fashioned a tent that could take the weather.

Stetson made a hat for himself using the same felt-making method. Leaving a big air pocket between the top of the head and the hat's crown for insulation, Stetson's first hat also sported a wide brim to keep out water and the sun. He tried to make the inside waterproof so that the hat could double as a water bucket in an emergency. The term "10-gallon hat" originated with the Stetson though the original never held more than a half-gallon of liquid.

A passing bullwhacker, driving his yoke of oxen, saw the hat and recognized its serviceability. He bought it for a five-dollar gold piece. Stetson realized that others would benefit from a wide-brimmed hat that would protect them against the rain and sun. People soon discovered other advantages of "The Boss of the Plains." Fleas had trouble finding a home in the hat's tough felt, unlike the infestations commonly found in coonskin caps. The Stetson hat is also tough, keeping its shape after intentionally being hit by 20 bullets.

When Stetson opened his first hat factory in Philadelphia in 1865, he was the sole employee. By 1885, Stetson owned the world's biggest hat factory, employing nearly 4,000 workers. At the time of Stetson's death in 1906, the factory was producing about 2 million hats a year.

The hat became a symbol of the American West, conjuring up images of cattle drives along the old Chisholm Trail. Many famous people wore Stetson hats, including Col. George Custer, Buffalo Bill Cody, Annie Oakley, Wild Bill Hickok, and Calamity Jane. In Hollywood westerns, Stetsons became icons of good (white hats) and bad (black hats).

Stetson's success is a prime example of the axiom: *"Necessity is the mother of invention."*

CHAPTER 17

Entrepreneur/Gelatin

Rose Knox

When Rose Knox's husband died in 1908, everyone wondered what she would do with the couple's gelatin company. That is, everyone except Rose Knox. Few women worked in businesses during this time, and Knox was 50 years old. Surely she would have a son take over the family business. Not Rose Knox. Instead she took the helm and turned Knox Gelatine into a food staple that revolutionized gelatin cookery.

Born in Mansfield, Ohio, in 1857, Rose Markward married Charles Knox in 1883. Wanting financial independence, the couple decided to start their own business. Knowing that many women used gelatin for cooking, Charles and Rose figured that if they could provide a quicker and easier way of making gelatin, they'd have a viable product. Together they devised the first pre-granulated gelatin.

With $5,000, Rose and Charles Knox started a prepared gelatin business in Johnstown, New York. Rose cooked and tested recipes then spread the word about cooking with gelatin by handing the recipes out to friends, neighbors, and local grocers. She held cooking demonstrations. Slowly the Knox Gelatine Co. was built.

When Charles died in 1908, their company was the largest gelatin maker in the U.S. Rose was determined to retain control of the business, despite the fact that a businesswoman from the middle or upper classes was unheard of at the time. She sent cards to the company's customers and clients announcing her husband's death, and stated that the couple's elder son, Charles, would take over his father's responsibilities. Few knew that Charles was still in school. The ruse was successful.

Knox worked deftly to garner her employees' support and loyalty. On her first day as president, she had the back door to the plant closed. "We are all ladies and gentlemen working together here," she announced, "and we'll all come in through the front door." In 1913, she instituted a five-day workweek along with two weeks' paid vacation a year and paid sick leave. Throughout the Great Depression, she achieved her goal of not having to lay off one employee. Eighty-five percent of the company's retirees had been with Knox 25 years or longer and most retired on pensions.

Knox shifted many of her husband's ad campaigns, which had aimed primarily at men. Common sense told her that gelatin was bought and used mainly by women, and attracting their attention would generate greater sales. She knew that women would be interested in easy-to-prepare food with high nutrition at a low cost. Hundreds of recipes were printed on Knox packages, on fliers, and in cookbooks. Knox also distributed a free column to newspapers called "Mrs. Knox Says," which included recipes and cooking tips. The column became so popular that women began writing her for advice—not just on gelatin, but on anything from farming to choosing a husband.

Knox kept pursuing growth. In 1916, she bought into the company that provided Knox Gelatine with its raw material. Once she realized that people were adding flavors to gelatin, she built a second plant in Camden, New Jersey, in 1936, to produce flavored gelatin.

Through her success, Knox made sure that she had the support of her community. She was a beloved benefactor of the local high school, churches, YMCA, and Johnson Hall State historic site. She was also responsible for establishing a sports field and a home for elderly women. Knox had a custom of giving a rose to each graduating high school senior girl and an orchid to every bride in Johnstown. She became known as "First Lady of Johnstown" due to her generosity. In 1937, Knox was voted the woman who had contributed the most to American business by the New York State Federation of Business and Professional Women.

Knox was still the company's chairman when she died in 1950, at age 93.

Rose Knox summed up her philosophy as such: *"All I've had to guide me is just plain common sense, and in dealing with people I've always tried to remember that molasses catches more flies than vinegar."*

CHAPTER 18

Daring/Courage

Admiral William F. Halsey

A surprise attack at Pearl Harbor on December 7, 1941, caught the U.S. off guard. Naval leaders needed to strike a blow that would stall the Japanese advance in the Pacific and restore American morale.

Vice Admiral William F. "Bull" Halsey, commander of the aircraft carrier USS *Enterprise*, had the answer: ignore conventional wisdom. Halsey directed his force deep into the Japanese-held Marshall Islands in January 1942 and launched airstrikes at enemy naval bases. Launching 21 airstrikes, he caused heavy damage on ships and planes. "We did the exact opposite of what the enemy expected," wrote Halsey in his autobiography. He took the battle to the enemy instead of engaging it at sea.

Halsey's fleet helped turn the tide of World War II. Halsey said, "If any principal of naval warfare is burned into my brain, it is that the best defense is a strong offense."

When U.S. forces were struggling against the better-equipped Japanese at Guadalcanal Island in October 1942, Admiral Chester Nimitz put Halsey in charge. His task was to fight off the Japanese in order to keep the U.S.-held airfield, a key to the American supply lines. Halsey fought for what he believed in, and he had the supreme confidence that the valor and ability of his men would surpass that of the enemy. He never let his men believe that they would fail. "For his effect on morale, Bill Halsey is worth a division of battleships," Nimitz told reporters.

The Japanese were trying to deliver enough firepower to expel the American troops from the airfield. Halsey had to block the bigger Japanese fleet. In the fierce five-day battle that ensued, Japan lost 16 ships with nine damaged. The U.S. lost 10 ships with seven damaged but won a decisive victory. Japan never seriously threatened the island again, and the U.S. seized the offensive.

Halsey became the navy's go-to guy in a crisis, because he threw himself into each challenge with gusto. His spirit was evident from early on, when he was trying to win an appointment to Annapolis at age 15. He wrote to every politician he knew and many he didn't. He even wrote to President McKinley. After two years of trying, Halsey decided that if he couldn't get into the navy as a cadet, he would as a doctor. He enrolled at the University of Virginia to study medicine before receiving an appointment from McKinley the following spring.

Halsey ran a tight ship, but he earned the loyalty of his men by treating them with respect. He relied heavily on their decision making and tried to keep regulations to a minimum. He called sailors by their first names and permitted officers to forgo their neckties. Halsey wanted a clear understanding of a pilot's problems and mental processes. So at age 52, he became the oldest person to win Naval Aviator's Wings. Halsey also became one of only four men to attain the rank of five-star admiral. He died in 1959 at the age of 77.

CHAPTER 19

Determination/Swimmer

Gertrude Ederle

Nineteen-year-old Gertrude Ederle was bitterly disappointed when pulled from the freezing waters of the English Channel on August 18, 1925. Just seven more miles and she would have completed the 21-mile swim from France to England.

Hundreds had attempted the arduous channel swim before Ederle. Only five men had made it all the way. Swimmers in its ice-cold waters were subjected to powerful currents, wind and fog. It brimmed with jellyfish and Portuguese men-of-war and occasionally was visited by sharks. If this weren't enough, the swimmers also had to avoid the giant freighters in the channel, the world's busiest shipping lane.

Ederle returned to America after her failed attempt. She spent the next few months plotting a new attempt. She hired Thomas Burgess as her new swimming coach. He was one of the five men who had completed the channel swim, although it had taken him 14 tries. Ederle knew she would have to build mental toughness for her rematch against the sea. She also planned a bold departure from tradition. Instead of the breaststroke, which was used by all five successful channel swimmers, Ederle decided to try a new stroke called the crawl.

Ederle's next attempt to cross the English Channel took place on August 6, 1926. She wore a red bathing cap, a two-piece bathing suit and goggles. She slathered herself with olive oil, lanolin, petrolatum, and lard to protect against jellyfish and cold. Ederle entered the 61-degree water at Cape Gris-Nez, France, at about 7 A.M. London bookies had set 5-1 odds against her making it.

Two boats accompanied Ederle during her attempt. She could often be heard singing, setting her strokes to the beat of the music. When the weather turned fierce and 20-foot swells battered her, she combated her fears by listening to the reporters' off-key renditions of "Yes, We Have No Bananas" and "East Side, West Side."

Hours into the swim, Ederle's left leg grew numb, and she had trouble kicking. The sea swells and currents had become so powerful that for every yard she progressed, she was pushed back two. Both her father and her coach pleaded with her to come out of the water, but Ederle refused. She had decided she would finish the swim or drown.

At 9:40 P.M., after more than 14 hours, Ederle reached the shores of Kingsdown, England. Hundreds of people holding flares were there to cheer her. Ederle had beaten the men's record by more than two hours. Her record would stand for 24 years. Making her feat even more amazing is that experts estimated that she had swum 35 miles to cross the 21-mile channel, due to the rough waters.

Ederle's "don't quit" philosophy helped her win three medals at the 1924 Olympics and to set 29 U.S. and world swimming records. She inspired more than 60,000 women to earn American Red Cross swimming certificates during the 1920s. When somebody would tell her she couldn't do something, that's when she would do it.

CHAPTER 20

Organizer/Scouting

Juliette Low

At a time when women were supposed to accept their place in the home, Juliette Low (1860-1927) traveled wherever she wanted. Playful, adventurous and curious, the Southern belle would try anything from flying an early airplane to welding iron to make a gate for her country estate.

As a widow on a trip abroad, Low met British-born Sir Robert Baden-Powell, founder of the new Boy Scouts movement, and his sister, Agnes, who with him had founded the Girl Guides. Low was fascinated. She thought girls in the U.S. could have fun learning to tie knots, signal to one another and start a fire from sticks.

In 1912, such pursuits were thought to be unladylike. Undaunted, Low decided to start the Girl Scouts in the U.S. She wanted girls to enjoy the same outdoor experiences that she had, so she traveled the country gaining volunteers and publicity. In Chicago, she spoke to a group of service leaders. In Baltimore, she persuaded Cardinal Gibbons to let her form troops in Roman Catholic settlement houses. She went to Washington, D.C., and was able to attend a meeting at the White House. Knowing that President Woodrow Wilson was the honorary president of the Boy Scouts, Low thought that the First Lady could get behind the Girl Scouts in the same way.

By 1915, the Girl Scouts had 5,000 members who paid 25 cents a year in dues. The Girls Scouts went on to become the largest not-for-profit organization for girls in the world. More than 43 million American girls have participated in Girl Scouts. Today, membership exceeds 3.6 million.

Low wrote a handbook that showed girls how to earn merit badges. She adopted the Boy Scout motto "Be Prepared" and stated that the Girl Scout purpose was "To do a good turn daily." She encouraged the troops to enjoy the outdoors and stressed sportsmanship, teamwork and fun meetings. Members of the first American troop, in Savannah, Georgia, played basketball in bloomers, such a risqué endeavor that the girls had to curtain off the court to passersby.

Low had quite a knack for securing reluctant but crucial volunteers to her cause. Being partially deaf, Low would pretend not to hear any reasons why someone could not serve. "She simply smiled at you and said, 'Here are the girls. You will start at once.' You were swept along in her train," said one friend. The praise she lavished on her volunteers kept most of them on board, and donations poured in. She made the organization community based, with each local office in charge of their own finances, training and recruiting.

In her later years, Low was rarely seen out of her Girl Scout uniform, her whistle and knife dangling by the side. She was buried in her uniform, as a brigade of Girl Scouts stood by as guards of honor.

Low never lost her original vision of Girl Scouts: The girls must always come first.

CHAPTER 21

Faith/Charity

Mother Teresa of Calcutta

It was 1948 when Sister Teresa, then 38, received permission to leave her religious order to go to work in the worst slums of Calcutta, India. She paid no attention to her colleagues when they said she'd never make a dent in the misery and poverty in Calcutta, let alone the world. Two years later, she founded the Missionaries of Charity in Calcutta, a religious order whose main purpose is to serve the poorest of the poor. Her bold effort started a movement. At the time of Mother Teresa's death in 1997, members of the Missionaries of Charity were in more than 100 countries. They serve millions of people crippled by poverty, illness, and rejection.

By focusing on the task at hand, Mother Teresa opened 500 orphanages, soup kitchens, AIDS hospices and other institutions around the world. "Don't look for spectacular actions," she said. "What is important is the gift of yourselves. It is the degree of love that you invest in each of your deeds."

As a young girl in Skopje, Macedonia, Agnes Bojaxhiu—Teresa's name before she became a nun—learned a lot about giving to others from her mother, Drana. A widow, Drana Bojaxhiu supported her three children by putting in long hours at her embroidery business. In spite of her workload, Drana always seemed to find the energy to help other people. Lazar Bojaxhiu, Mother Teresa's elder brother, remembered their mother hearing of a woman who had a tumor and no one to care for her. Despite all of her other responsibilities, Drana housed and fed the woman and cared for her until she got well.

Dinner table talks in the Bojaxhiu home usually centered on teachings of the Roman Catholic Church, Bible reading, and the activities of the missionaries throughout the world. Young Agnes absorbed it all like a sponge. She loved to meet the returning missionaries and hear their accounts of work in the field. Agnes felt her calling, and at age17 set her sights on becoming a nun in India. The next year she left for Dublin, Ireland, to join the Loreto Sisters, a missionary educational order, and never saw her mother again.

When in Dublin, Agnes learned English and honed her spiritual know-how. In 1931, she became Sister Teresa and took a job teaching history and geography at St. Mary's School for Girls in Calcutta. For the next 17 years, Sister Teresa threw herself into her job and worked to become the best teacher she knew how to be. While riding on a train in September 1946, she felt a call to form her own religious order. "I heard the call to give up all and follow Christ into the slums to serve him among the poorest of the poor," she said. Before she could strike out on her own to form an order, though, she had to get permission from the church.

The clergy in Calcutta told Sister Teresa that she would have to stop being a nun altogether if she wanted to work solo. She refused to accept that, so she went on writing and rewriting letters to everyone from Pope Pius XII to the archbishop of Calcutta to the mother general of the Loreto Sisters. Her persistence paid off. In 1948, Sister Teresa received permission to prove herself. She was given one year to show the church that she could do it on her own.

In December 1948, Sister Teresa started with what she knew best. Approaching a small group of children, she traced the ABCs in the mud with a stick. Delighted, throngs of the poorest children she had ever seen gathered around her, eager to learn the alphabet.

The school she opened became the first of many triumphs. In 1950, she received permission to found her order, the Missionaries of Charity. In 1952, she opened a home where the dying could go for comfort, and in 1957, she opened a home for people afflicted by leprosy. Her successes did not come without strife, however. Once, when asking a baker for some bread to feed the poor, the baker spat in her face. Undaunted, she calmly replied, "That's for me—now how about some bread for the poor?" The baker complied.

Mother Teresa received numerous honors for her works, including the Nobel Peace Prize and the Congressional Gold Medal.

"No matter who says what, you should accept it with a smile and do your own work."—Mother Teresa

CHAPTER 22

Inventor/Basketball

James Naismith

In 1891, as a teacher at the International YMCA Training School in Springfield, Massachusetts, James Naismith was given two weeks to invent a safe indoor sport for students to play during the cold winter months. Gym classes at that time tended to be regimented calisthenics, gymnastics and drills, and the students were restless for active games they could play indoors. At first he tried to bring sports like baseball, cricket, football, lacrosse and soccer inside. There simply wasn't enough room inside for baseball and cricket. Lacrosse, football, and soccer were too rough and dangerous, especially on a hardwood floor. Naismith didn't give up. With one day left, he asked himself: Why not take segments from different sports to make a new one?

Naismith (1861-1938) envisioned a game in which players would pass the ball to each other with the ultimate goal of scoring points. He decided that football was the logical place to start. But he had to eliminate running because the gym was small, and tackling wouldn't do because of potential injuries. Naismith then considered a game he played as a child called "duck on the rock." The object of the game was to throw rocks to knock a small rock off a larger one. The most successful players lobbed their stones with an arc, rather than throw them hard like a line drive. Naismith viewed his new game the same way, where accuracy would be more important than force.

Naismith still needed to figure out what the goal would look like. He recalled competing in a game where the objective was to throw a rugby ball into an empty box on the floor. But scoring was almost impossible because the defenders crowded around the box, sometimes even climbing into it. Naismith's solution was to have a goal above the floor so defenders couldn't divert the ball so easily.

Naismith selected a soccer ball for his new game and asked the janitor if he had any wooden boxes to be used as goals. The janitor offered him two peach baskets he had in his storeroom, which Naismith accepted. He hooked a round peach basket 15 inches in diameter onto the lower balcony on each end of the gym. He put the baskets 10 feet above the floor, and divided his gym class into two teams of nine. The positioning of the players was derived from lacrosse.

On December 21, 1891, the first organized basketball game took place in Naismith's school gym. It ended in a 1-0 score! Realizing that the floor was limited in size, Naismith reduced the number of players to seven then to the current five. His height for the baskets remains the same today. Most of his original thirteen rules have been modified, but the spirit of the game remains the same.

The sport was an immediate success, catching on in hundreds of YMCAs and colleges around the world. Naismith became the father of basketball, and the National Basketball Hall of Fame in Springfield is named for him. Naismith not only discovered the solution to his problem of keeping students in condition during the winter months, but also created what has become one of the most popular team sports in the world today.

Naismith's game of basketball is a prime example of how most inventions are derived from pre-existing elements. It just takes a special individual to know how to combine them.

CHAPTER 23

Leadership/Warrior

Geronimo

It was 1851. Apache warriors had finally tracked down the Mexican army raiding party that had slaughtered most of Geronimo's village, including his wife and three children, three weeks before.

Geronimo (1829-1909), then a young warrior named Goyakla, had been chosen to lead the attack. But the fight was going badly, and the Apaches were suffering heavy losses. As more and more Apaches fell to the Mexican guns, the outcome began to look bleak. To inspire his warriors, Goyakla threw himself into the battle, fighting hand-to-hand with Mexican soldiers in a small wooded area until he was the only one standing. His actions energized his fellow warriors, and they regrouped to claim victory. As the battle turned against them, the Mexicans desperately cried out "San Jerome!"—praying to St. Jerome to save them. The Apaches, mistakenly mocking their cries, called out "Geronimo!" The name stuck to their leader, Goyakla.

Growing up in what is now New Mexico, Geronimo was trained for survival from a young age. Tribal leaders made the boys rise early every morning and ran them for hours to increase their endurance. They learned to make bows, shoot rifles and race ponies to increase their hunting ability. In addition, Geronimo learned wrestling and tracking, and he knew every inch of the land around his home. To strengthen himself for long runs in the desert, he scaled mountain passes with his mouth full of water without swallowing any of it to learn to breathe through his nose. He also dodged arrows shot at him in order to quicken his reactions. At age nine, to test his survival skills, Geronimo was left in the desert without food or water. Because of his thorough training, he was able to find his way home in three days.

Famed Chief Mangas Coloradas recognized Geronimo's battle skills in his first raid, on a band of Mexican soldiers. After the fight the chief designated him a warrior. The Apaches soon had a new force to deal with once the U.S. had defeated the Mexicans in 1848. American settlers began to move into Apache lands, and the Apaches were determined to retain their hunting grounds. Even during the ensuing battles with the settlers, Geronimo tried to behave with integrity. He instructed his warriors to avoid hurting the settlers whenever possible and told his men to refrain from stealing because it would diminish them as warriors.

In 1871, Congress attempted to end the frequent skirmishes by moving the Apaches to reservations. Conditions on the barren reservations were horrific. There was no vegetation or animal life, so the Apaches had to depend on food supplied by government contractors. Often, that food was rotten meat. The Apaches resisted fiercely, but by 1873, great leaders like Mangas Coloradas had been killed and others like Cochise had surrendered. But Geronimo refused to live in the poor conditions of the reservation.

In 1881, Geronimo took a raiding party of several hundred warriors and escaped the San Carlos Reservation in the Arizona territory. He kept his warriors motivated by leading them in group prayer to the Great Spirit and talked about the importance of working together. Despite being on the run from government forces, the Apaches flourished under his leadership. Knowing the army was tracking him, Geronimo would throw off the government scouts by splitting his group into small parties. He would have his groups weave across each other's tracks, meeting for a day or two then splitting off again. He would march for miles down streambeds in order to leave no tracks. When his pursuers did get close, Geronimo would set the desert grass on fire to slow the pursuit and give the Apaches time to escape.

After constant running for nearly five years, Geronimo felt it was the best decision for his people to finally surrender. Life on the run was hard, and the Apaches and their horses often went without water for days at a time. Geronimo knew that continuing would eventually lead to their death.

Knowing that the government had broken treaties before, Geronimo was wary of making any new agreements. He carefully questioned a junior officer to determine whether his pursuer, Gen. Nelson Miles, could be trusted. Geronimo posed only seemingly obscure questions such as, "Does he look you in the eyes?" "Do the officers trust him?" "Does he have many friends?" Only after Geronimo was satisfied with Miles' character did he agree to surrender. Geronimo continued to try to help his people. He traveled to Washington and tried to persuade President Theodore Roosevelt to return his homeland.

Gen. Nelson Miles said of Geronimo, *"He was one of the brightest, most resolute, determined-looking men that I have ever encountered."*

CHAPTER 24

Innovator/Bicycles

Ignaz Schwinn

By 1895, there were 90 bicycle manufacturers in Chicago. The saturated market had companies operating on razor-thin margins. This did not stop Ignaz Schwinn from entering the game. He had a strategy. He had watched what customers liked, and he had figured out how to give it to them.

Schwinn decided to pursue the high end of the market. He would build strong yet light first-class bicycles and hire only bicycle enthusiasts as salesmen. Schwinn insisted on using only the best steel and production equipment. The promotion method he decided on was to develop a track record of excellence in bicycle racing. The publicity would surely increase a demand for his bicycles.

Schwinn spent a lot of time on the road recruiting bicycle enthusiasts to be his salesmen. He also watched countless races to find the right racer to be his spokesman. In 1896, he signed an emerging star from Minneapolis, Joe Johnson, to represent Schwinn and ride only his bikes in races. To make sure Johnson reached his potential, Schwinn hired as his coach the best-known trainer of cyclists in the U.S., Thomas Eck. Whenever Johnson and Eck won, Schwinn bought full-page ads in cycling publications to promote his bicycles.

Born in Hardheim, Germany, Schwinn saw the bicycle evolve from the high-wheeler of the 1870s to the "safety bicycle," which had two wheels of the same size. Using his experience from working in bicycle shops, Schwinn drew up plans for several models of the safety bicycle. His attempts to sell his designs failed initially, as manufacturers still favored the high-wheeler. His persistence eventually paid off when he was able to convince the owner of Kleyer Bicycle Works to manufacture his designs. By 1887, Schwinn was the manager of Kleyer Works, overseeing the production of safety bicycles.

In search of greater opportunities, Schwinn moved to America in 1891. He soon landed the superintendent's position at Hill Cycle Manufacturing Co. in Chicago. Schwinn knew he had the experience to go into business for himself, but he lacked capital. He looked hard for a partner, and was eventually able to secure financial backing from meatpacker Adolph Arnold. Their partnership lasted from 1895 until 1908, when Schwinn bought Arnold out.

The automobile ended the bicycle boom, but Schwinn had kept a keen eye on trends and was quick to expand into the next hot area: motorcycles. His Excelsior-Henderson operation became one of the Big Three in American motorcycle making. By diversifying, Schwinn was able to keep his bicycle business going during the industry's most difficult period, from 1900 to the 1930s. Staying afloat during the tough times also created great loyalty from his employees.

When the Great Depression ended the motorcycle boom, Schwinn closed that line of business and moved his motorcycle engineers into his bicycle works. He assigned them the mission of improving the bicycle quality and appearance at the lowest cost. Schwinn saw that children were the new target market. His new strategy was to make the Schwinn bicycle something that every child would want.

Schwinn introduced the "Streamline Aerocycle" in the mid-1930s. The Aerocycle's streamline design was the first departure from the standard industry bicycle design in 40 years. The traditional thin tires were replaced with Germany's automobile-like, double-tubed "balloon" tires. Schwinn's ability to understand his customers' wants helped

Schwinn to become the most recognized name in the U.S. bicycle industry.

CHAPTER 25

Passion/Musician

Ludwig Van Beethoven

In 1802, at age 32, Ludwig Van Beethoven was steadily losing his hearing. He had tried everything his doctors had prescribed, but nothing worked. The thought of being unable to compose music due to deafness had Beethoven considering suicide.

But Beethoven's passion for music inspired him to fight his depression and continue composing. By doing so, Beethoven (1770-1827) went on to become one of the all-time greats. Beethoven wrote, "Ah, it seemed impossible for me to leave this world until I had brought forth all that I felt was within me."

Beethoven was familiar with struggle. As a boy he did not have an easy life due to an abusive father. As a 4-year-old he started studying both the violin and piano. Sadly, Ludwig was often beaten or locked in the basement by his father in order to make him practice. Sometimes, after coming home drunk, Ludwig's father would wake him and make him play music until the morning.

Despite his father's overly strict teaching methods hampering his progress, Ludwig still showed enough talent to be noticed. Bonn court organist Christian Gottlob Neefe took over his training in 1780, when Ludwig was 10. Neefe gave him regular instructional hours, showed patience and provided encouragement. Beethoven blossomed under his new teacher; publishing his first compositions at 11 and directing the court orchestra part time by age 12.

To further refine his skills, Beethoven decided to move to Vienna where he began studying under Joseph Haydn. Beethoven's early work under Haydn pleased his teacher very much. However, as time went on Beethoven's creative will started to clash with Haydn's classicism. Beethoven's work tended to emphasize feeling and emotional range, going away from classical to romantic style. Despite Haydn's insistence, Beethoven refused to write "pupil of Haydn" on the title page of his works because he wanted to make sure people knew he was a composer in his own right. When he decided that Haydn's exercises were hurting his development, Beethoven moved on.

Confident in his abilities, Beethoven began playing the piano at social functions throughout Vienna to make a name for himself. By 1795, he was playing in local concerts and even made a European tour the next year. Beethoven used bigger orchestras for his symphonies than other composers had in order to give audiences a wider feel for the music. He changed tempo frequently to give his music more energy. He even used instruments to mimic songs of birds he heard on his daily walks.

Though bewildered at first by its new elements, audiences eventually embraced Beethoven's musical style. Once he wrote ideas down, he wouldn't stop working until the music turned out just right. "The working out begins in my head, and since I know what I want, I hear and see the work in my mind in its entirety." Beethoven typically ignored critics of his work, but if the criticism was universal he was willing to change. When his opera, *Fidelio*, closed after only three performances in 1805, he read the reviews and asked his friends and colleagues for their opinions. He worked hard to revise the opera, even dropping an act. The improved version opened the next spring to far warmer reviews and is now considered one of the finest operas ever.

Beethoven composed nine symphonies, six overtures, thirty-two piano sonatas, nineteen sonatas for strings, seven concertos, one opera and numerous smaller works. "I live entirely in my music," he wrote to a friend in 1801, "and hardly have I completed one composition when I have already begun another. At my present rate of composing, I often produce three or four works at the same time."

Beethoven realized that his success was due to his love for his work and a total focus on its production.

CHAPTER 26

Creator/Painter

Grandma Moses

Anna Mary Robertson Moses' rheumatism made it difficult to do her usual farm chores and housework. Being 77, there seemed to be little hope of finding a cure. Her doctors told her that if she could find a way to keep her hands flexible, the pain might ease.

Moses had been interested in the art of painting. It seemed it would be a good way to keep her hands moving. Her self-guided physical therapy proved a boon for the rest of the world. Better known as "Grandma Moses," she became America's best-known folk-art painter.

She painted scenes she knew, such as her farm and landscapes. Few appreciated her work at first. When she entered her paintings in a local fair, she also entered her canned fruits and raspberry jam in a contest. Her fruit and jam won prizes, but her paintings did not.

Moses (1860-1961) didn't get discouraged. She continued painting simply because she loved to paint, often working on more than one piece at a time. About the time of the fair, art collector Louis J. Caldor saw Moses' paintings displayed at a local drug store. He was impressed and bought many of Moses' paintings. He took them to New York to show, but they failed to spark interest in others. Caldor still believed in Moses. He bought her painting materials of a more professional quality and encouraged her to continue.

Otto Kallir, the owner of a new art gallery, became interested in Moses' paintings. He was struck by the landscape of one of her paintings. "The landscape was painted with astonishing mastery," Kallir recalled. "Though she had never heard of any rules of perspective, Mrs. Moses had achieved an impression of depth . . . creating an atmosphere of compelling truth and closeness to nature." Kallir sponsored Moses' first exhibition in October 1940 with 34 paintings. One of the first paintings sold was to Thomas J. Watson Sr., the mastermind who built IBM Corp. and who became Moses' friend.

Presidents Truman, Eisenhower and Kennedy honored Moses. She also corresponded with Winston Churchill, a fellow amateur painter. By completing more than 25 paintings after her 100th birthday, Moses was able to show that age needn't be a barrier to productivity. And she did it all without ever taking a painting lesson.

Born in Greenwich, New York, Moses had lived modestly on farms all of her life. She was the mother of 10 children, although five did not survive infancy. Moses was a perfectionist. "Painting is a very pleasant hobby, if one does not have to hurry. I love to take my time and finish things right," Moses wrote. She didn't paint to please dealers or agents. She painted to please herself.

Moses didn't understand or seek the attention that came from her painting. She was practically immune to the virus of fame and self-importance. "People tell me they're proud to be seen on the street with me. But I just say, 'Well, why weren't you proud to be seen with me before?' If people want to make a fuss over me, I just let 'em, but I was the same person before as I am now," Moses said in 1940.

Moses chose to stay positive through her art and to use it to cheer others up. *"I made the best out of what life offered,"* she wrote, *"And life is what we make it, always has been, always will be."*

CHAPTER 27

Entrepreneur/Engineer

An Wang

An Wang started his business with just $600 to his name. The business grew into Wang Laboratories, a $3-billion computer company.

Wang (1920-1990) was born in Shanghai, China, but was reared in a small village. At the time, China was feeling the turmoil associated with the growing revolution. Warlords were gaining control after thousands of years of imperial rule.

At age 6, Wang started in the third grade, as there was no first or second grades in his small village school. He thrived at the challenge of competing against the older children. Math was Wang's favorite subject, but his study of the English language allowed him to learn about the outside world. Wang's parents chose to send him to one of China's best secondary schools where he continued to flourish. His entrance exam score for admission to Shanghai's Chiao Tung University was the highest in his class. There he studied electrical engineering and translated articles from American science magazines.

In 1937, Japan invaded China. Wang's mother, father, and sister died during the war. Despite the situation, Wang graduated at age 20. He aided the Chinese war effort by designing radios for the troops. By 1941, Japanese-occupied Shanghai wasn't safe. Wang and many other students fled deep into the countryside seeking refuge.

After the war, Wang and several other engineering students went to the U.S. on two-year apprenticeships. Their aim was to learn Western technology to be used in the rebuilding of China. Wang attended Harvard University, earning a master's degree in applied physics in 1946 and a doctorate in applied physics and engineering 16 months later. His success landed him in the Harvard Computation Lab, home of the Mark I, one of the first computers.

Wang was asked to research information storage, and in 1949, he invented a magnetic memory core. His invention allowed computers to save data to a device that would allow for more complex calculations. Later that year he married and filed for his first patent.

Wang Laboratories was started in June of 1951 in an empty South Boston building. Wang started selling his memory cores and his business took off. He continued to improve his cores and actively marketed new uses for them. One of the first digital scoreboards at New York's Shea Stadium was programmed with the cores. In 1965, Wang introduced the first desktop calculator, bringing the power of big mainframe computers to a single desk. Scientists and engineers clamored for the device.

Wang's next calculator design, the Model 300, was designed for business people. It also was a great success and Wang Laboratories continued to boom. In 1964, Wang employed 35 people; by 1967 there were more than 400 on the payroll. Knowing his success with calculators wouldn't keep the company profitable forever, Wang began plans to design and market computers.

Magnetic core memory was followed by the semiconductor chip, which had much greater memory storage capacity than the cores. Realizing the impact that this small chip would have on the computer industry, Wang was the first customer of Intel Corp., a company that sold the chip. In 1970, Wang introduced the word processor, a real godsend to secretarial workers everywhere. The personal computer was his next hit.

Wang became a benefactor of many causes with his wealth, donating money to Harvard and founding the Wang Institute. His money built an outpatient unit in Massachusetts General Hospital, and his $4 million gift allowed the repair of Boston's performing arts center. Wang Laboratories suffered economically in the early 1980s, and the different divisions were sold off to relieve the debt. Wang died of cancer at age 70 in 1990.

An Wang believed that to succeed you need to find a need and fill it.

CHAPTER 28

Inventor/Kool-Aid

Edwin Perkins

Edwin Perkins (1888-1961) invented over 100 food products, but by far his biggest selling was Kool-Aid. Devised in the mid-1920s, Kool-Aid has be a rite of childhood for more than 70 years. Today, Kool-Aid is consumed at the incredible rate of 17 gallons per second during the summer months, undoubtedly aided from sales by young entrepreneurs and their neighborhood stands.

Perkins displayed an enterprising spirit at an early age, wanting to sell a product for an honest dollar. Growing up in the small town of Hendley, Nebraska, Perkins relied on mail order to cultivate his aspirations. He saw a newspaper ad, "How to Become a Manufacturer," and sent in his money for the information. He studied the guide intently and started experimenting in his mother's kitchen. Once he had created a few perfumes and flavoring extracts to sell, Perkins realized that he now needed labels. He sent in for a small hand press that he had seen in another newspaper ad. Not only did he make his own labels, he let the townsfolk know of his purchase and that he was open for business. By the time he was in high school, Perkins was the only printer in town.

Perkins continued to cultivate his mail-order business while editing and publishing the local newspaper and serving as village postmaster. His products included a quit-smoking remedy called Nix-O-Tine, insect killer, flavorings, spices, and grooming preparations. Inspired from attending a household products seminar in St. Louis, Perkins came up with a name for his line of products-Onor-Maid. Though sales were good, Perkins was still searching for a best-selling product. Finally, in the mid-1920s, Perkins emerged from the kitchen with a new creation he called Fruit Smack. He knew he liked it, but he wanted to test it on family members. They gave the sweet and fruity drink mix rave reviews, so he immediately added it to his line of products. There were problems with the new product, however. Fruit Smack was a liquid concentrate sold in 4-ounce glass bottles. These were costly to ship and often broke in transit.

Perkins studied the problem and decided the drink mix would be better sold as a powder. He dried the drink out and started combining dextrose, citric acid, tartaric acid, flavoring and food coloring. After many attempts, Fruit Smack became an easy-to-ship powder. Perkins renamed the product to Kool-Ade in 1927, and trademarked the name Kool-Aid in 1934. Kool-Ade came in strawberry, cherry, lemon-lime, grape, orange and raspberry flavors, and at 10 cents a packet, was a bargain that all families could enjoy.

Perkins next task was to make Kool-Ade easy to sell. Rather than market it by mail order or door-to-door sales like his other products, Perkins decided to sell Kool-Ade through wholesalers to retail grocery and candy stores. Kool-Ade was a hit, and Perkins struggled that summer to keep up with the orders. He developed the "Self-Selling Silent Salesman," a point-of-purchase display containing 40 1-ounce envelopes of the six different flavors. This carton sat open on any countertop, and helped launch Kool-Ade without much capital.

In 1933, in the thick of the Great Depression, Perkins cut the price of Kool-Ade from 10 cents to 5 cents a packet. The impact on the company was enormous, as sales increased from $383,000 in 1931 to $1.5 million in 1936. Once the rationing of fruit acid and dextrose ended with World War II, demand for Kool-Aid skyrocketed. By the 1950s, 300 workers were turning out a million packets each day. Kool-Aid is still one of the most recognized products on U.S. grocery shelves.

Edwin Perkins' determination and drive helped him turn Kool-Aid into a household name.

CHAPTER 29

Inventor/Lego Toys

Ole Kirk Christiansen

It was 1931, and Denmark's economy was sinking. Ole Kirk Christiansen faced a tough decision. Should he continue as the best builder in town or set out on a new path? He had just let go the last worker in his carpentry firm and was raising his four young sons alone since his wife had died.

Despite the hard times, Christiansen (1891-1958) refused to give up. He took the advice of the local Chamber of Commerce to start producing household goods. In 1932, he opened a firm, renamed Lego in 1934, that manufactured stepladders, ironing boards and toys. Sales languished for the ladders and ironing boards, but the wooden toys were a hit with the customers. People loved the fine detail, sanded edges, smooth surfaces and beautiful layers of varnish of the toys.

But Christiansen saw potential in a new material—plastic. Despite objections from his sons, in 1947 Christiansen purchased a costly injection-molding machine for plastics. That investment revolutionized the way children play with toys. Lego has grown into a household name throughout the world, employing 10,000 people in 30 countries. Between 1949 and 1998, Lego had produced an astronomical 203 billion plastic Lego elements.

After much trial and error, Lego churned out its first plastic toys in 1947, including a baby rattle shaped like a fish and a highly popular farm tractor. By 1949, Christiansen oversaw production of 200 different toys. His sons, who all worked at the firm, still tried to persuade Christiansen not to use plastic. They pointed out the heavy costs and how hard it was to get raw materials. They pleaded for him to return to wood, but Christiansen wouldn't give up his vision.

Christiansen figured that the way to success would be to focus on the company's best product. At a 1954 toy fair in Britain, a toy buyer told him that the problem with the toy industry is that there is no system to anything. Christiansen determined that he already had a toy with an inherent system—his Automatic Binding Bricks. He shifted his focus to improve the product from every angle. He wanted the product to spur a child's imagination and creativity, one that could be played with over and over again. The concept helped persuade retailers to put the toy on their shelves.

In 1955, the firm came out with its first Lego System product, Town Plan No. 1. Children could build houses on top of a large plastic sheet detailed with roads, crosswalks and signs. That same year, Lego came out with twenty-eight different play sets and eight vehicles. Supplementary brick elements were also sold to enhance the overall system.

Though sales were good, Christiansen received a number of complaints from customers that the bricks did not stick well together. His commitment to quality forced Christiansen to challenge his engineers to come up with a way to improve the clutching ability of each brick. The company lab tried ribs and grooves, but the improvement was minimal. Finally, in 1958, the engineers placed three tubes in the bottom of each eight-stud brick. This did the trick, and the firm secured a Danish patent for the design.

To market the Lego System globally, the firm sponsored building competitions with prizes to lure children in their shops. Christiansen refused to lower the quality of his product line to save money. Lego factories insist on accuracy to the thousandths of a millimeter, evidence that their high-quality standards exist to this day.

Lego's success is well summed up by Christiansen's favorite motto: *"Only the best is good enough."*

CHAPTER 30

Perfectionist/Violin

Antonio Stradivari

A ntonio Stradivari wanted his violins to be perfect. To do this, he would take weeks or even months to produce a single instrument, at a time when many artisans could turn out a new instrument every few days. As a result, his instruments are looked upon as works of art, and even today are considered benchmarks of quality. Of the more than 1,100 stringed instruments he produced in the latter 1600s and early 1700s, about 650 still exist.

Their high quality was no accident. Stradivari (1644-1737) was entranced by the sound of the violin at an early age. When he was 13, he began studying its shapes, sounds, materials, varnishes and music. He studied violin making in Cremona, Italy, under the tutelage of Nicole Amati, the last member of a family famous in the craft. Stradivari stayed with Amati's studio until about the age of 40, even though he had earned the right from the musician's guild to print his own labels at age 16. Doing so allowed him to focus on the details of making the instruments rather than running a business.

He learned as much as he could from Amati and any other craftsmen he happened to meet. He also spent a great deal of time studying alone in the workshop, examining the best violins he could find, and trying earnestly to duplicate them. He threw out imperfections or any piece that did not meet his high expectations. It has been said that he threw out nearly half of what he made.

No detail was too small for Stradivari's attention. He experimented with every aspect of the instrument until he found a sound that would please him. He honed his skills until he could cut out a pattern freehand that was mathematically correct. He based the style of his violin on Amati's design, only smaller and more responsive. By the late 1670s, his style was quickly becoming popular with musicians. He continued his efforts and perfected his "Long Strad" design in 1690. It was the culmination of years of experimentation with the smallest details in shape, size and materials.

After leaving Amati's workshop, Stradivari worked on the flat roof of his house. He was able to hang his newly varnished instruments out to dry during favorable weather. This unusual aging and drying process was part of his formula for the superior tone of his instruments.

As word spread of his skill, people came to watch him working. Stradivari encouraged this free advertising, knowing it would lead to commissions. Among the many who commissioned his instruments were James II of England and Charles III of Spain.

Stradivari continually experimented with minor details in his pursuit of perfection, particularly when it came to varnish. He used a secret formula that helped his instruments resonate their distinctive tone. His varnish was derived from beeswax from the Cremona area. It remains unparalleled in imparting visual and tonal beauty.

Stradivari died in his house in Cremona at the age of 93. A plaque dedicated to his life stands on the wall of his home. It says, *"Here stands the house in which Antonio Stradivari brought the violin to its highest perfection and left to Cremona an imperishable name as master of his craft."*

CHAPTER 31

Rehabilitator/A.A.

William Wilson

When William Wilson (1895-1971) was two years old his hard-drinking father left his family. Bill's mother was forced to move the family from Vermont to Boston. She had her parents tend Bill and his sister while she went to medical school.

In childhood, Wilson was in a constant state of illness. The stigma of a broken home and the death of his high school sweetheart were challenges he faced. But he didn't give into depression; he instead looked for ways to improve himself.

He joined the military, and used his time to analyze where he was headed. By the time he was discharged, he'd come up with a life plan. He decided to study law, but started drinking heavily. Once, he was too drunk to take the tests. He managed to get his degree and headed for Wall Street.

He learned to pick stocks, and soon had more money then he'd ever seen before. He drank more than ever. His career survived the October 1929 crash because of a friendship with a Canadian businessman. After a few months he was fired for drinking; by 1933, Wilson and his wife were living on charity in her parents' house. He had become an unemployed drunk who hated religion and had sunk to panhandling for cash.

At his lowest point, he was visited by an old drinking buddy. Now sober, this friend told him of a method that had worked for him. His method maintained that the key to sobriety was a change of heart with an admission of powerlessness, a moral inventory and surrender to a higher power. To reform was to take responsibility for past deeds and to make amends, not only for the sake of the person he might have wronged, but to restore pride in himself.

Wilson was impressed when he saw his friend sober and happy. He decided to try it. He stopped drinking, remembering how he felt with hangovers. Spending a year tracking down old acquaintances, he took personal responsibility for his life. Even after gaining a new job, the battle was not easy. Once, when a sales deal fell through, he could hear the sounds of the bar calling. He felt a need to drink.

But he knew he couldn't. He telephoned an old drinking buddy, Dr. Robert Smith, who was a drunkard, and talked to him for hours about the havoc it wreaked on lives. Wilson focused on helping Smith. If he could stay sober by talking to someone else, maybe others could be helped too. Smith had his last drink on June 10, 1935, the official birth-date of Alcoholics Anonymous.

This strategy helped others and was a necessary part of staying sober. Among the steps to stop drinking was service to others. To convince others that they would be safe in his program, no one would use last names. Participants would promise to not repeat stories that they heard in meetings.

Wilson, for his success, refused to be honored publicly by declining an honorary degree from Yale or an appearance on *Time Magazine's* cover. He died in 1971.

CHAPTER 32

Inventor/Plastics

Leo Baekeland

Leo Baekeland (1863-1944) invented a new printing paper that allowed photography to use artificial light to print images. But professional photographers dismissed Baekeland's product called Velox. They preferred to expose film negatives slowly to strong sunlight over several hours to make a print.

Baekeland was not discouraged. He looked to the younger generation, as the amateur photographers weren't stuck in the past. They would be more likely to want to try something new. So he geared his advertising directly at them. Baekeland placed step-by-step instructions on the paper containers on how to use his method. With gas or electrical lighting, prints could be made any time of the day.

His strategy worked. Following directions on how to use the paper achieved good results. As Velox caught on, George Eastman, the founder of Eastman Kodak Co., bought the rights to Velox for between $750,000 and 1 million in 1899.

Baekeland was born the son of a shoemaker in Ghent, Belgium, in 1863. His father wanted him to improve his lot by reading and study. At age 8, Baekeland read a translation of Benjamin Franklin's autobiography. He connected with its theme that with thrift, energy, and ingenuity, a poor boy could rise to great wealth and high position. He took an interest in chemistry and photography. By age 17, he was one of the best scholars in Ghent. Eventually becoming assistant professor of chemistry at the University of Ghent in 1882. But Baekeland felt that America offered greater opportunities. Working for a photographic supply maker, he saw what sold and what didn't.

He struggled in his earlier years and became ill. "I committed the mistake of scattering my attention on too many subjects at the same time and it dawned on me that I had too many irons in the fire." He decided to concentrate on just one thing, which resulted in Velox.

Financially well off at 35, he traveled to Europe and learned of new chemical processes. Back in Yonkers, New York, he converted a stable in the backyard into a home laboratory. He wanted to develop a new electrical insulator to replace shellac. He tried different approaches to find a synthetic shellac. After 5 years, he invented Baklite, the first plastic that did not soften when heated. He worked for 18 months more to refine the process. The material broke easily. He tinkered with the formula adding fillers to make it less brittle.

The new plastic was introduced at the New York meeting of the American Chemical Society in 1909. Samples included billiard balls, pipe-stems and potholders. He organized General Bakelite. By 1939, Bakelite was used in automobile engines, airplanes, propellers, toasters, radio cabinets, hair brushes, phones, pens, and electrical plugs.

Moral: Baekeland didn't let close-minded people get him down.

CHAPTER 33

Visionary/Scientist

Michael Faraday

Michael Faraday (1791-1867) had vision and determination. His development of the principles of the generator and electric motor paved the way for modern civilization.

Born in London, Faraday was one of 10 children in a poor, uneducated family. Attending school, he learned basic reading, writing and arithmetic. He knew nothing about advanced mathematics. When he turned 14 he went to work for a book binder. For the next seven years he read books on science and chemistry.

When Faraday didn't understand something in a book, he would ask questions when no one could answer his questions. He conducted experiments and built his own equipment. He also built his first electrostatic machine. His hard work and inquisitive attitude paid off. In 1812, Faraday received tickets to attend a lecture at the Royal Philharmonic society. The speaker was Humphry Davy, a famous chemist and teacher.

Taking extensive notes, he called on Davy for a position at the Royal Society. Davy had no job available, but interviewed him anyway. Davy was impressed and hired Faraday. When a job opened up for a chemical assistant in 1813, Faraday worked hard conducting experiments. Around 1820, Danish physicist Hans Christian Oersted discovered the relationship between magnetism and electricity. Davy and Faraday grew interested. After many failed experiments, Faraday demonstrated that an electromagnetic current caused a magnet to revolve around a wire carrying current. These movements continued as long as the current continued to flow. Here was the principle of the electric motor. For the next 10 years, he kept on experimenting until the summer 1831, when he hit on a new idea. He took a coil of insulted wire, connected it to a galvanometer, and wound the coil onto a hollow paper cylinder. As he pushed the magnet into and out of the cylinder, the galvanometer registered an electric current passing through the coil. In further experiments in October 1831, he made a copper disk rotate between the poles of a large magnet. He had built the first generator, the principle upon which commercial electricity is produced today.

Faraday was an independent thinker. He joined a very small and despised sect of Christians known as the Sandemanians. He married Sarah Bernard, a member of one of the leading Sandemanian families. Sandemanian faith asked him to lead a plain devoted life, and so he stayed humble. He turned down the presidency of both the Royal Society and the Royal Institution. Refusing knighthood, he said. "I must remain plain Michael Faraday to the very last."

Moral: Faraday had vision and determination to reach his goals

CHAPTER 34

Pioneers/Flight

Wilbur and Orville Wright

On December 17, 1901, Wilbur Wright (1871-1912) and younger brother Orville Wright (1867-1948) realized their vision of human flight at Kill Devil Hills sand dunes at Kitty Hawk, North Carolina. As youth, they loved to tinker with mechanical things. When bicycles became popular, the brothers opened a bicycle shop in Dayton, Ohio. At the time scientists, the press and the government doubted that man would ever master motor-driven flight. The *New York Times* wrote that a man-carrying airplane would take millions of years to reach that point.

Wilbur and Orville Wright studied the great diversity in shape and size in birds. They figured humans could fly if they developed the know-how. Reading books, pamphlets and talking with others increased their interest. They sought advice from Samuel P. Lanley, whose great Aerodrome had crashed into the Potomac river. Aviator Octave Chanute gave advice on double deck wing design. They scoured the findings of Otto Lilienthal, who had developed the correct wing curvature that produced lift.

They figured that human flight depended on a way to control the aircraft. Spending afternoons lying on a hill, they watched birds fly. They watched buzzards tilt the end of one wing up and the other downward. This motion allowed them to make sweeping turns. The brothers designed a set of wires connecting the wing tips of the airplane so as to manipulate the wings angles to the wind. In 1809, they built a glider that flew for 15 to 20 seconds for about 400 feet.

During the winter of 1901, they made a 6-foot-long wooden air tunnel testing miniature airfoil air pressure and wing span. In 1902, they built a new glider with a wingspan of 32 feet. It spun out of control one in every 50 flights. While lying in their tent on the dunes at night, Orville realized that the answer was to have a single vane tail connected to the wing warping wires. The pilot could now control both wings and tail.

That did the trick; they made hundreds of perfect glides at Kill Devil Hills. A year later in 1903, they staged several motor-driven trips above the dunes. Using an engine they had built themselves, they made two hand levers so that the pilot could separately control the rudder and wings. In 1906, an upright seat was installed where previously the pilot lay prone. By 1909, wheels replaced skids.

To gain recognition, they took to the skies in France and Germans flying over huge crowds. They were spurned by the U.S. Army at first, but by 1908, the Signal Corps bought a plane that could fly 40 mph and carry two men and supplies for a distance of 125 miles. The Wright Brothers developed the Vin Fiz, which completed America's coast-to-coast flight in 1911.

CHAPTER 35

Entrepreneur/Avon

David Hall McConnell

David Hall McConnell grew up on a farm in Swego, New York. He learned to work hard tilling the fields, but McConnell (1858-1937) wanted to make more than just a good living, so he figured that would involve leaving his father's farm to do it.

His first job was as a book salesman for a New York company. Naturally sociable, he would tailor his pitch to what interested his customers. After just a few months, his bosses made him a general agent, which he worked at for the next three years. After accomplishing all that he could with that company, he went to work for Union Publishing Co. After just three years, he was placed in charge of the entire southern territory with headquarters in Atlanta.

Experience as a canvasser and general agent gave him good insight into human nature. He said, "I learned to be practical and how to sell goods to the consumer." McConnell started handing out small perfume samples to encourage housewives to listen to his book sales pitch. The customers were more interested in the perfumes than in his book.

He decided to quit the book business and start a line of perfumes. He asked women what their favorite scents were and then found books that told him how to make perfume. McConnell set up a small space in New York City and created the little dot perfume set. It consisted of five fragrances: white rose, violet, lily of the valley, heliotrope, and hyacinth. The first batch didn't cover half the cost of the raw materials. Realizing he had to fine-tune his recipe to get the maximum scent for a minimum price, he stayed up late at night to experiment until the recipes were perfect. Eventually he was able to produce fragrances as fine as other perfumes.

Searching for a name, he decided to name his venture the California Perfume Company. To make his fragrances the best, he hired a man who had a great reputation making perfumes. Realizing that he needed a woman's touch, he hired Mrs. P.F.E. Albee, a dynamic agent whom he had worked with in the book business.

Her advice: hire women to sell as they were more likely to trust each other. Recruiting women, Albee used the pitch that they could earn pin money in their spare time while providing a lady-like service. McConnell produced a catalog showing his products. To control quality, he built a laboratory in 1897 at his home in Suffern, New York.

Within two years, business at the California Perfume Company was growing rapidly. As his customer base grew, he branched out into toiletries, shampoo, creamy balm, and toothpaste. The first color catalog of his products was printed in 1905. He advertised in *Good Housekeeping Magazine*. The California Perfume Company earned its first million dollars in 1920. Two years after his death in 1937, the company's name was changed to "Avon" after William Shakespeare's home Stratford-upon-Avon, England, an area he thought resembled his own countryside.

Moral: You can build a better mousetrap, but it will go nowhere without a good marketing plan.

CHAPTER 36

Patriot/Statesman

Alexander Hamilton

Alexander Hamilton was born out of wedlock on the Caribbean island of Nevis in the British Indies in 1775. The family moved to St. Croix in the Virgin Islands when he was about 10. His father abandoned the family in poverty there, and his mother died when Hamilton was 13.

Lacking money, connections or prestige, he knew he would have to work for everything. Hamilton was ambitious and wanted to be successful. He found a job as a clerk with a trading company. He was like a sponge and soaked up every experience and was soon promoted because of his dedication and hard work.

St. Croix was the center of the slave trade where the slaves were treated miserably. This fostered Hamilton's anti-slavery sentiment. He wanted to keep learning. His drive impressed a local minister who raised funds to send Hamilton to school in the American colonies. Arriving in New York City in 1772 or early 1773, Hamilton began his studies at Kings College (now Columbia University). He had heard of events leading up to the Boston Tea Party. To learn more, he traveled Boston to see for himself the situation first hand. Deciding the Colonies' cause was just, he couldn't wait to take part as war broke out. Hamilton joined a New York artillery battery. Reading everything he could find on the subject, he was accepted as a captain taking part in significant battles with GeorgeWashington guiding his troops to strategic locations cutting off British forces.

His skill impressed Washington, and he was made an aide-de-camp in 1777. At the end of the year, Washington sent him to request additional troops from Horatio Gates. Wanting to palm off a weaker brigade, he insisted on stronger one and got it.

In 1782, Hamilton studied law and was admitted to the New York Bar. Once his office was opened, he represented anyone whose case was just, even if they had been a Tory Loyalist. The treaty of Paris stipulated that at the end of the war neither side would persecute citizens who had taken opposite sides during the war, yet some British loyalists had not been given back their property. Hamilton knew this was wrong and was dedicated to justice.

Hamilton resisted efforts to run for national office, but played a role at the Constitutional Convention. Ultimately the Constitution won approval, and Washington then became the nation's first president. Washington appointed him secretary of the Treasury.

Resigning office in 1795, he went into private law practice. During this time he incurred the wrath of Aaron Burr who challenged him to a duel. Hamilton opposed dueling but accepted the challenge. On July 11, 1804, Hamilton was wounded by a single shot. He did not fire his weapon at Burr. He died the next day.

CHAPTER 37

Advocate/Reformer

Elizabeth Kubler-Ross

Elizabeth Kubler-Ross had just obtained her medical degree from the University of Zurich, Switzerland, in 1957 and was full of optimism about treating patients. What she saw made her furious. Terminally ill patients were being abused and ignored.

Patients were placed in rooms far away from nursing stations and forced to lie under bright lights they couldn't shut off. They were denied visitors, except during certain hours, and deceived about their medical condition. They were mostly left alone to die.

Kubler-Ross was determined to change this, no matter the cost. She challenged the medical community and became a voice for the sick. Her motto was "To avoid criticism say nothing, do nothing, be nothing," a saying that hung on her wall.

As an advocate for the terminally ill, she lectured to educate medical personnel on the needs of dying patients. Changes were slow in coming as the physicians weren't embracing her approach. She decided to let dying patients speak directly to her audience. Patients agreed and told of their ordeals. Some physicians tried to prevent her from visiting patients, some nurses called her a vulture, and her assistants were treated like lepers.

Kubler-Ross remained unfazed, forging ahead with workshops, seminars, and counseling of the ill. She urged peers not to mislead patients about conditions. She was convinced that honesty was the best policy. She used criticism as a fuel to drive her campaign. The more honestly and concisely she gave prognoses, the better patients were able to handle their illness.

As a psychiatrist, she visited terminally ill patients in their hospital rooms and homes. Sitting beside them she would say, "Tell me what you're going through." She identified five stages of emotional preparation for death: denial, anger, bargaining, depression, and final acceptance.

Her studies convinced her that terminally ill patients should be permitted to die at home, surrounded by loved ones and familiar sights—even those requiring extensive medical attention deserved to spend their final days in a quiet, comfortable, and compassionate setting. These convictions convinced Kubler-Ross to become one of the founders of the American Hospice movement. In the early 1990s, she had grown concerned that babies with AIDS were not receiving good care. Medical workers treated them with fear. She planned to make a hospice for AIDS babies at her ranch in Virginia. Neighbors telephoned, wrote letters, and signed petitions to protest. Tires were flattened, her house was broken into, and shots were fired through her windows. Arsonists burned down her home and killed her pets. Moving to Arizona, she still refuses to give up her life's work. Her challenges, setbacks, and hardships are lessons that she says though painful, result in growth.

CHAPTER 38

Explorer/Seaman

Samuel de Champlain

Samuel de Champlain was born and raised in Brouage, a seaport on France's west coast. His father was a captain in the French Navy, and his uncle was a ship commander. Absorbing their advice, he became an excellent seaman. Tales he heard from sailors inspired him.

On one occasion, Champlain saw three Indians, who had been captured in Canada and taken to France, being prodded with a sword before a laughing crowd. Champlain knew it was wrong; he then had an overwhelming desire to go to Canada. In 1599, his uncle invited him to go to the West Indies. It would be his first transatlantic voyage. Champlain (1567-1635) detected an abundance of fruits and animals and suggested they be used for trading. In Panama, he recognized that a canal across the Isthmus would speed freight to the Pacific Ocean.

He learned native customs, made paintings and sketches of his sightings and, when returning to France, drew 62 maps. He also was a store of information on the flora, fauna, mines and systems of government.

Soon after, Champlain met Aymar De Chaste, owner of a fur trading monopoly in Acadia, Canada. Invited to help lead a trading expedition to Canada, Champlain saw it as a great opportunity.

Reaching Canada in 1604, the expedition sailed up the St. Lawrence River where he mapped the area. Returning to France, he gave a complete report to King Henry IV.

In 1608 he returned to Canada several times. One time his party of explorers had to forage in the woods to eat. The fierce Iroquois tribe repeatedly attacked. Making friends with the Montagnais tribe, he led a charge against the Iroquois. One time an arrow hit him in the ear and buried itself in the neck. Unfazed, he ripped it out and continued to fight. Champlain decided in 1608 that a permanent settlement would help his explorations. He looked for a site with rich soil and easy access to the ocean and inland waterways. At the mouth of the St. Lawrence River, he founded Quebec. Champlain established fur-trading networks that would be the foundation for the colony's growth and prosperity. He sought to discover new minerals and soil for farming. He also laid out plans for a new harbor.

Without his persistence and willingness, New France would not have survived in America.

CHAPTER 39

Inventor/Helicopter

Igor Sikorsky

Experts in aviation laughed when Igor Ivanovich Sikorsky wanted to build a plane that flew vertically as well as horizontally.

Sikorsky (1889-1972) as a youth was excited by the stories of Jules Verne and the drawings of Leonardo da Vinci. At age 12, he built his first rubber band—powered model helicopter. It did not fly very far. When he was 14 he heard about Orville and Wilbur Wright's flight at Kitty Hawk, and he knew the direction he would go in his life.

To learn more later in life, he studied at the Russian Naval Academy in Kiev. In 1906, Sikorsky studied engineering in Paris. A year later, he went home to study at the College of Mechanical Engineering of the Polytechnic Institute of Kiev. There, Sikorsky worked on his idea of a helicopter, designing and experimenting on the aerodynamics for his helicopter. The experts said it would never work. Sikorsky remained undaunted. Using a motorcycle engine in 1909, he built a helicopter with coaxial twin-bladed rotors. The craft vibrated so much it rattled to pieces. After much experimenting, with successes and failures, he finally hit upon the right combination. In May 1911, he built his S-5 with a 50-horsepower engine that flew successfully.

The Russian Imperial Aero Club granted Sikorsky a license. The Russian Army found it to be faster than other foreign aircraft. Next came the S-21 airplane, which was nicknamed "The Grand," with an 89-foot wingspan and a gross weight of 9,000 pounds. When it flew on May 13, 1913, Sikorsky became the world's first four-engine pilot. A bigger bomber version took off in 1914.

Sikorsky was made a hero, but the Bolshevik revolution in 1917 made him an outcast. Rather than staying in Russia, he fled to New York in 1919. Relying on his experience, he found engineering work with the U.S. Army Air Service in Dayton, Ohio. That job fizzled out. He was flat broke. He taught math, astronomy, and aviation principals. Friends pooled their resources, and Sikorsky's Aero Engineering Corp. was born in 1923. Collecting surplus parts from army junkyards, he built the S-29A. Pan Am and United ordered planes.

Now financially secure, he built his new Sikorsky helicopter on September 14, 1939. Military contracts came pouring in. It surpassed all previous helicopter records because it was stronger and faster. Sikorsky retired in 1957. The company became a division of United Technologies Corp., which would bear his name. He died at age 83 in October of 1972.

CHAPTER 40

Inventor/Nylon

Wallace Carothers

Wallace Carothers (1896-1937) was born in Burlington, Iowa. As he grew, he loved to read. He studied the life of Thomas Edison, read the books of great authors, and loved the music of Bach and Beethoven.

Obtaining his chemistry degree, he developed his reputation as a chemistry professor at the University of Illinois and at Harvard. Then the opportunity presented itself in February 1927 to go to work at the Dupont Company as head of the chemistry department.

Carothers earned the respect of his staff. He encouraged new ideas. Carothers inspired loyalty by remaining modest and kind. He didn't micromanage his chemists, supervising them only enough to make sure they did not go off on a tangent.

During his nine years at Dupont, he and his research team invented the first synthetic rubber, Neoprene, in 1931. Then came the first synthetic silk nylon in 1934. The first uses for nylon were in toothbrush bristles and stockings. During World War II, nylon was the key to America's war effort. It was used for outerwear, tents, tire yarn, and parachutes. The U.S. Army floated to earth in Normandy on nylon. Carothers' invention of nylon marked the beginning of the modern era of scientific design of materials for the needs of mankind.

Neoprene was not a planned experiment. Team members expected to derive a liquid substance from a chemical mixture and instead got a rubbery one. Carothers theorized that polymer fibers were made up of long chains of repeating atoms. To prove his theory, he combined chemicals until he'd created spaghetti-like modules.

The polymers Carothers invented, that eventually became nylon, presented a major problem at first—it had to be heated in order to soften its sticky mass so that fibers could be made from it. But the heating caused melting, and the resulting fiber was charred and too brittle.

Through trial and error, Carothers realized that the molecule combination he was using to create the polymer created water as a by-product, giving the polymer too low a melting point. The team removed ethyl alcohol from the compound thereby eliminating the water. The result was a polymer that had a higher melting point of nearly 400 degrees Fahrenheit. As a result, nylon was much stronger than silk. In 1936, Carothers received the highest U.S. scientific honor by being elected to the National Academy of Sciences.

CHAPTER 41

Author/Children's Books

Horatio Alger Jr.

Horatio Alger Jr. (1832-1899) was the best-selling author of all time with more than 400 million books sold, more books than Dickens, Thackery, Hemingway, Falkner, and Douglas combined. Countless millions of boys and girls were influenced by Alger, and many gave him credit for their success.

Born in Revere, Massachusetts, he was the son of Horatio and Olive Alger. Never very strong—and asthmatic—he was seven years old before he learned to talk intelligibly, and even then he stuttered. When eight years old, his father, a Unitarian minister, gave him a Bible and started him off on the study of Greek, Latin and the classics. At thirteen, he entered Gates Academy. In 1848, he passed the entrance examination at Harvard, graduating in 1852. Between tours of Europe, he graduated from Divinity School in 1861 and was ordained a Unitarian minister. However, he was not cut out to be a minister, and in 1866, left for New York City.

Even before graduating from Divinity School, he had written his first book, *Bertha's Christmas Vision*. It had been published in 1856, followed by six other children's books. However, it was his eighth book, *Ragged Dick*, published in 1868, that propelled Alger to prominences as a writer of "rags to riches" stories for boys and girls. It received enthusiastic response from readers.

Throughout his life, Alger loved children and dedicated many of his books to them. He never maintained a house or apartment of his own but lived in the Newboy's lodging house and other boarding houses. Following upon the success of Ragged Dick came *Fame and Fortune, Mark the Matchboy, Rough and Ready, Ralph Raymond's Heir, Luck and Pluck, Sink or Swim, Ben the Luggage Boy,* and *Rufus and Rose.*

One of Horatio Alger's books had a notable social impact. His book *Phil the Fiddler* told the story of a young Italian street musician who was a victim of the evil Padrone system that had been exploiting young homeless, Italian immigrants unmercifully. As a result, new laws were enacted and steps taken to rid New York of the evil system.

In 1899, Alger turned 67. He was old and tired and suffering with bronchitis and asthma. He lived with his sister, Olive, and her husband, Amos, in south Natick, Massachusetts. He was virtually broke. The end came July 18, 1899.

Alger's writings, compared with today's standards, were mawkish and at times amateurish. Alger was unsurpassed in his day. It is notable that, over a hundred years after his death, he still has thousands of readers and fans. His books are rare and valuable collector's items. The Horatio Alger Society continues to promote his "rags to riches" theme that continues to inspire today.

CHAPTER 42

Inventor/Firearms

Samuel Colt

Samuel Colt (1814-1862), a native of Hartford, Connecticut, was fascinated with science from his youth. He earnestly studied chemistry and mechanics. As a boy, he figured out how to transfer an electric charge through a waterproof wire to set off an explosion. He was inspired by a story from the revolutionary war about a general who was armed with a double-barreled rifle.

If he could invent a gun that would shoot five or six times without reloading, it would rule the world. Colt's first two attempts to manufacture a multiple-shot gun failed.

In 1830, at age 16, Colt was sent to sea by his father to seek his fortune. Aboard the ship *Corvo*, Colt noticed that regardless of which way the steersman spun the wheel, each spoke came in line with a clutch that could be set to hold it. Inspired, he began envisioning holes in the rim which he saw as the bore of the pistol barrel. The idea of the revolver was born. Others had experimented with revolvers, but Colt's design was the first to rotate the cylinder automatically when the gun was cocked.

He had an idea but no money. Looking for a way to get cash, he decided to use his knowledge of nitrous oxide (laughing gas). Organizing a one-man sideshow, he demonstrated the effects of the gas on people. His demonstrations were a success. The crowds loved watching what nitrous oxide did to people.

At age 20, he gave up his sideshow and secured patents for his revolver. Colt's six-shot "peacemaker" was sabotaged twice and caused his Patent Arms Company to go bankrupt in 1842. Still he remained optimistic. Just before the bankruptcy, Captain Sam Walker of the Texas Rangers had bought one of Colt's revolvers. Walker and his fellow Rangers believed in the revolver. In 1846, Walker and Colt worked to make improvements that would make the gun indispensable on the American frontier. The U.S. government ordered a thousand guns, and with the profit Colt built a new factory in Hartford, Connecticut.

The Colt revolver was used in the Mexican War (1846-1848) with great success. Mexico blamed their defeat on Colt's six-shooters. In the 1850s, the Crimean War swept Europe, and demand was high for his guns. With increased orders, Colt expanded to England. By this time, Colt operated the world's largest private armory. He introduced standardized production, division of labor, and assembly line production. On the eve of the Civil War, he began production of a new lightweight .44 caliber army revolver.

Even after Colt died, his revolver played an important role in America's history. Colt revolvers were standard issue for military and law enforcement officers for more than a century. What he wanted wasn't money, but achievement to do what had never been accomplished by man.

CHAPTER 43

Entrepreneur/Tupperware

Earl Tupper

Earl Tupper (1907-1983) was born in Berlin, New Hampshire. He was a self-educated man. His passion for learning included studying such subjects as technology, marketing, and consumer trends.

Eking out a living in his tree surgery business during the Depression was difficult. He tried to stay positive and improve himself during the depressed economic times, but his tree surgery business failed in the mid 1930s. His real passion was inventing where he had little success. Inventing was really where his heart was rather than tree work. Tupper wrote down all his goals and monitored his progress throughout his life.

In 1937, Tupper landed a job at Doyle Works as a plastics prototype maker. In that job, Tupper saw how plastic could benefit the public. He soaked up all the knowledge he could on his own time. He developed his own small plastic products such as unique toothbrushes, tumblers, and combs. These he sold by mail order.

In 1938, he started Earl S. Tupper Co. manufacturing plastic goods and gift articles. He would do research at trade shows and fairs, asking questions of everyone. He asked for feedback from friends and family on his inventions. When World War II came, he made plastic parts for gas masks.

By 1942, Tupper was able to convert unrefined polyethylene into an odorless, non-greasy flexible, durable plastic. By trial and error he turned polyethylene into Tupperware. In 1946, the first Tupperware containers were marketed using ingenious airtight seals. Sales grossed more than $5 million in 1947.

Tupper's high-quality products were made in attractive translucent pastel and mineral colors to associate them with semiprecious stones; this he thought denoted quality and elegance.

After its first few years of sales in stores, he had failed to secure a stable consumer base. Searching for an answer, he hit upon holding neighborhood parties with housewives to sell goods. He was influenced how Stanley Home Products had succeeded. The power of these innovative products required demonstrating the virtually airtight resealable lids. By 1951, Tupperware products were pulled from retailers' shelves in favor of home parties. In 1958, Rexal Drug and Chemical Co. purchased Tupperware for $16 million. It is said that a Tupperware party takes place somewhere in the world every 2.5 seconds. By the year 2000, sales were $1 billion. Earl Tupper was inducted into the Plastics Hall of Fame in 1976.

CHAPTER 44

Inventor/Reading

Louis Braille

Louis Braille (1809-1852) was 3 years old when he climbed up on his father's workbench and picked up a sharp metal saw, even though his father had forbidden him to touch any tools. While trying to punch holes in a piece of leather, the saw slipped and plunged into his left eye. The left eye became infected, and infection spread to this right eye. By age 4 he was completely blind.

He seemed fated to become a beggar, but his parents knew he was a bright son and wanted him to be educated and self-sufficient. They insisted he do his chores by touch. Using his cane, his father made him memorize how many taps it took to get from one point to another. He found the stable by smelling the horses and hay, and the bakery from its aroma of fresh dough. He learned to identify voices, the swish of a woman's skirt, and different horse-drawn vehicles.

In 1815, a local priest began tutoring him verbally three times a week. Reading stories from the Bible, works of literature, and learning astronomy and other subjects, he memorized names, recited verses of poetry, and learned the scent of flowers, textures of things and songs of birds.

The priest helped him get into the village school where he soaked up everything. He could solve complex math problems in his head. But when it came time to read and write, he could only sit and listen. His family helped him learn the alphabet by shaping letters out of straw.

When he turned 10, he won a scholarship to the Royal Institute for the Blind in Paris. Students learned to trade and play instruments. Books were embossed with raised letters that students could read by touch. It was a slow process. Charles Barbier, a retired ship captain, had developed a code system consisting of raised dots and dashes in heavy paper, so French soldiers could send battlefield messages in the dark. In 1821, he brought his "Sonography" method to see whether blind students could use it. Louis was ecstatic; it was easier to read dots and dashes with his fingers.

Braille determined to improve upon the method. After many months of experimenting, he came upon a system of dots and dashes and reduced them to represent letters rather than Barbier's method based on sound. The school arranged for him to meet Barbier, who was insulted that a 13-year-old was suggesting changes in his method. Braille was discouraged at first but pressed on for the next two years. Braille cut the numbers of dots in each column from six to three and got rid of the dashes.

In 1821, at age 15, he tested his method in school while the school director read aloud, Braille punched out the words with his stylus. When the director finished reading, Braille ran his fingers over his page and read the story back aloud. Today Braille's alphabet is the universal reading method for the blind.

CHAPTER 45

Inventor/Television

Philo T. Farnsworth

Philo T. Farnsworth (1906-1991) was born in Beaver, Utah. His father was a farmer who often moved his family in search of more fertile planting ground and better opportunities. Moving to Rigby, Idaho, in 1919, young Philo found a pile of old science radio magazines in the attic left by the previous owner. As an avid reader, he would read late into the night. The next day, he would think about what he had read as he plowed the field.

One article was about a unit of electricity called an electron. Another was an article titled "Pictures That Could Fly through the Air." As he plowed the field one summer in 1920, Farnsworth looked back over the long, even rows he'd made with a harrow. He deducted that, using electrons, he could scan a picture row after row, from left to right, as one would read a page of print. This would create constantly changing electronic images.

Farnsworth enrolled at Brigham Young University in 1923. He found his teacher skeptical of his concept. After his father died in 1924, he had to leave BYU because he lacked money to continue his education.

Farnsworth wrote letters to wealthy people outlining his idea and received some support. Later Philco Radio Corp. came through with financial help. Always experimenting and recording notes on everything he did, he began memorizing his processes. With financial backing in place, he moved his lab to San Francisco. Picking his staff, he knew it was more important that each employee understand his vision and share it, keeping his lab informal. He conducted meetings casually. He wanted to encourage original ideas. When someone came to him with a problem, he'd supply just enough information to get the person thinking.

Farnsworth was never greedy. If a staff member developed a patentable idea, he'd help them get the patent. He inspired young inventors to never give up. If one of his men said the job was impossible, he would say to just give it more time.

On September 7, 1927, he transmitted the first clear TV picture on a 4-inch screen. When he started designing his first television in the mid-1920s, he had his notes signed, dated and witnessed. He had a feeling he might be challenged one day over patent rights; he was right. Radio Corporation of America had most of the patents on radio. Anyone who wanted to build a radio had to come to RCA.

In May 1931, RCA president David Sarnoff learned about Farnsworth's television design and offered to buy it for $100,000. Farnsworth wasn't interested in selling. Instead he wanted to license the design to others to generate funds for research. In 1932, RCA sued Farnsworth, claiming he'd stolen their ideas.

Farnsworth, a Mormon, had spiritual beliefs that carried him through tough times. He had faith that a higher power was guiding him. The courts ruled that Farnsworth's ideas were original thoughts based on his vast store of dated, signed notes. Finally, RCA was forced to negotiate in 1939, and a cross license agreement gave rights to Farnsworth's designs.

At the time of Farnsworth's death in 1971, a television receiver carried approximately 100 of his patents. He was the father of television with over 1 billion in use today.

CHAPTER 46

Composer/Music

John Phillip Sousa

John Phillip Sousa was born in 1854, in Washington, D.C. He studied the violin and trombone. When he became 13 years old, he left school to join the U.S. Marine band. He was named director in 1880.

After 12 years in the band, Sousa decided to start his own band. He knew the odds of succeeding were against him. No traveling bands of the day were profitable. Most of them failed after a few months on the road. But Sousa believed he had the talent and savvy to make a civilian band work.

During the next 40 years, the band traveled more than a million miles and gave more than 15,200 performances to audiences throughout the world. To set himself apart from other bands, he became a master publicist so much that he was compared to showman P.T. Barnum. By the late 1890s, he had achieved his dream. He was the best-known musical entertainer in the world. His fiery marches included "The Stars and Stripes Forever," "Semipro Fidelis" and "El Capitan." His music became synonymous with American patriotism. In the post-civil war America, it was unpatriotic to criticize him.

Souza was an upstanding role model. He despised swearing, drunkenness and bigotry. In public and private, he behaved like a well-mannered, likable person. Professionally, he was punctual in attendance, meticulous in dress and striking in military being. He stood so ramrod straight that people thought he was wearing a corset. He treated people with courtesy and made a point of addressing people warmly.

To bolster his image, he encouraged photographers to take pictures of him horseback riding, boxing, bicycling, and trapshooting. The press churned out announcements about Souza's band so much, that when he came to town there was a great excitement and magic. Flags were hoisted, businesses declared days off, schools recessed, and town officials met him at the railroad station with keys to the city.

Few could match his composing abilities. He wrote 336 musical pieces (including 136 marches), 332 musical arrangements, 7 books, 138 magazine articles, and 27 letters to the editor. During performance intermissions, he would be found working on new compositions instead of chatting with band members. Sometimes Sousa would surprise audiences by playing ragtime.

Because Sousa showed how committed he was to the music, the musicians put forth their best efforts for him. If a band member made repeated mistakes, Sousa would visit the man in private and make gentle conversation. Those who were under stress with personal problems would be given time off with pay, so they could resolve their difficulties.

In 1921, Sousa fell of his horse, breaking his neck. He took 10 weeks off to recuperate, and led the public to believe he only broke his arm. During his first performances, he refused to let the audience see him in pain. Sweat streamed down his face, and he left the stage in exhaustion. For Sousa, the show had to go on. He died in 1932, in Reading, Pennsylvania, a musical legend.

CHAPTER 47

Entrepreneur/IBM

Thomas J. Watson

Thomas J. Watson (1874-1956) was a born salesman. Because of his initiative and loyalty, he would rise to become president of International Business Machines, which is better known as IBM. His birthplace was Campbell, New York. He attended college in Elmira, New York, and held a variety of jobs before joining National Cash Register Company (NCR) in 1895. Soon after, he became general sales manager, which impressed President John Patterson.

It was not long before Patterson saw Watson as a threat to his position; Patterson fired Watson in 1913. He was unemployed for several months, but he remained optimistic by networking and pounding the pavement until he landed his position as head of Computer-Tabulating-Recording.

From the beginning, he set a goal to be loyal to his workers. He figured they, in turn, would be loyal to him. During the Depression, for example, instead of laying people off, he put on additional staff and increased production. When the economy turned around, he was ready for the major contract to provide machines for the Social Security Administration in 1936.

Watson opened a school to teach customers how to use the company's products. He believed that managers should be judged by the qualities and abilities of the people who work for them. He believed that men are pushed up, not pulled up.

Probably Watson's most famous dictum to his employees was "Think." He believed that those who didn't think had cost the world millions of dollars. He encouraged employee training and also built a new engineering laboratory. He insisted his salespeople look and dress alike but approach sales in a way that reflected their personalities. Present your sales proposition in your own way. Talk it over naturally as you would a friend, and you will make good in sales.

Watson tried to minimize turnover by emphasizing five points: hiring, training, supervision, promotion and firing, with attention to the first four points; the fifth point would be less likely. He tried to have an environment that encouraged promotion from within. He often cited examples of personnel who started at the bottom and rose to top positions at IBM.

During World War II, he limited IBM's profit to 1.5 percent on war contracts. In the 42 years Watson was at the helm of IBM, sales increased each year—from $4 million in 1914 to $570 million in 1954.

IBM was one of the first companies to offer workers fringe benefits such as health insurance, life insurance, and pension plan.

CHAPTER 48

Authors/Fairy Tales

Jacob and Wilhelm Grimm

Brothers Jacob Grimm (1785-1863) and Wilhelm Grimm (1786-1859) were born in Hanna, Germany. Their early life was difficult. Grimm's father, Phillip, died of pneumonia when they were at a young age. Mother Dorothea Grimm had only a tiny savings account. She decided that education would be the top priority for her children. Her children studied at home and later were able to attend Lyzeum, a prestigious high school in Kassel. There they graduated at the top of their classes.

Jacob and Wilhelm studied law on a scholarship at the University of Marburg. Realizing that language and culture are the keys to law, they began studying German literature and folklore. They put all their efforts toward understanding the words and stories of the German people.

In 1806, well-known folk song compiler Clemens Brentano hired them to do research on a coming volume of German folk tales. Logging hundreds of hours, they invited German peasants to tell tales passed down from generations of folklore. The brothers Grimm corrected, translated and edited 49 tales for Brentano. Meanwhile, Brentano had encountered personal problems and abandoned the project without even glancing at their hard work.

The brothers decided to keep on gathering tales and write the book by themselves. By 1812, they had 86 stories which became a book titled *Children's and Household Tales*. By 1858, after seven revisions, the book had a total of 210 stories.

Stories included in the book were "Cinderella," "Sleeping Beauty," "Snow White," "Little Red Riding Hood," and "Hansel and Gretel." The book has been translated into 160 languages. By the beginning of the twentieth century, *Children's and Household Tales* was second only to the Bible as a best-seller in Germany, and it has held that position up to the present.

Their work has thrilled generations of children. The Grimm brothers were successful because they went after details. They began recording every single work spoken by their sources. Rather than jotting down highlights and reconstructing the tales later, they tried to capture the tales verbatim. If the storyteller ended with the phrase "they lived happily ever after," those exact words went into their notebooks.

When Wilhelm recorded Marie Muller's version of "Sleeping Beauty," Muller said that everyone in Sleeping Beauty's castle fell asleep. He asked her, "Who exactly fell asleep?" She replied, "Even the flies on the wall fell asleep." This level of detail brought the story of life.

The Grimm brothers went to outlying farms and spinning rooms of peasant women. That's why many of Grimm's tales involved spinning wheels and flax. They collected stories from Germany, Austria, Switzerland, Denmark, the Netherlands and Belgium. By the 1870s, their book was used to teach reading all over Germany. Their legacy lives on today.

CHAPTER 49

Innovator/Nike

Bill Bowerman

B ill Bowerman (1911-99) was one of the greatest track and field coaches in the U.S. His credits include 24 National Collegiate Athletic Association individual campaigns, 4 NCAA team champions, 64 All-Americans, and the 1972 Olympic track and field team. Bowerman loved running. He wanted others to find the same enjoyment.

Bowerman was the head track and field coach at the University of Oregon from 1948 to 1972. He was very competitive and at the same time fascinated with the psychology and dynamics of running. He observed that runner's shoes were cumbersome. One morning in 1971, he observed his wife making waffles. As she poured the waffle mix into the waffle iron, he hit upon an idea. He was looking for a way to improve his athlete's performance. He mixed synthetic rubber into the waffle iron and let it cool. It took some work to get the rubber off the grill. When he finally did, he had come up with the first lightweight sole, the waffle sole, which revolutionized the running shoe.

Bowerman tested his shoes on his team members, including Phil Knight who would play a key role later on. Bowerman would sit in his garage and tinker with shoe designs, which he continued to test on his runners.

He figured others would be happy to have the shoes, too. In 1964, he and Knight teamed up to found Blue Ribbon Sports, Inc. In 1972, they started the Nike brand. That year, four of the top seven finishers in the Olympic marathon wore Nikes. The company name was changed to Nike, Inc. in 1980.

Based in Beaverton, Oregon, its products are sold in over 100 countries with over $8.8 billion in sales in 1999. Bowerman's inspiration and high standards set Nike on the road to success. He had a laser focus to solve a problem with an athlete and then move on.

Phil Knight was good at marketing and recognized the potential of the shoe designs, while Bowerman would pursue excellence at the company's board meetings. Knight remembered when he would criticize so much. A lot of times, it was a bit of a pain to have a board meeting interrupted by him saying how bad the product was. Over time, Knight came to believe that Bowerman was Nike's most valuable asset. He stood up for what he believed in and believed that the company had to keep improving to stay ahead.

Bowerman led by example, making education his No. 1 priority and training as No. 2. He hated being called "coach" and insisted on being called Bill. His love of running encouraged jogging classes for people of all ages. In 1967, he wrote a book outlining the joys and benefits of the sport. He helped develop rubberized asphalt runways for track and field events, providing a surface safer than grass. He made sure his team wore clothes of the lightest weight.

He believed that every ounce removed from the shoe's weight would save 200 cumulative pounds for a runner in a one-mile race.

He believed that victory is doing the best you can and, even if you lose, you will have learned something. He insisted that athletes undertrain in order to prevent injuries and reserve strength for the race. His idea was to work out hard one day, then light the next day, preventing injuries. Bowerman's innovations helped build the empire that Nike is today.

CHAPTER 50

Pioneer/Aviator

Amelia Earhart

On the morning of July 2, 1937, in Lae on the island of New Guinea, Amelia Earhart started the engines of her Lockheed Electra. She listened for a moment to their deep-throated roar, a sound she had once likened to poetry, and then pointed the silver plane down the runway. Heavily laden with more than one thousand gallons of fuel, the Electra lumbered toward a rocky sea embankment that marked the runway's end. Less than 50 yards from the precipice, Earhart lifted her plane into the air. It started to dive momentarily and then began to make a steady climb in the clouds.

Earhart and her navigator Fred Noonan were bound for Howland Island—a 2,556-mile journey and the longest leg of the flight around the world. Those who turned out to watch her departure from Lae were the last ever to see her.

Born in Atchison, Kansas, in 1897, the daughter of an alcoholic railroad lawyer and a genteel mother, Earhart was born with a para-devil streak, often doing things that boys did. At 21, she was working as a nurse's aide in a hospital in Toronto tending the wounded of the World War I. In November of 1918, she went to a local airfield and determined that she would one day learn to fly.

During the next several years, Earhart held more than 20 jobs including photographer, truck driver, and social worker.

Her first notable flight was as a passenger on a 1928 flight across the Atlantic with two male pilots. Other firsts include: first woman to fly solo over the Atlantic, first woman to fly solo from Hawaii to California, first woman to fly solo from the United States to Mexico City, first woman to make a transcontinental non-stop flight, and first woman to reach an altitude of 14,000 feet. Earhart was the author of three books and became well known on the 1930s lecture circuit, sometimes making as much as $2,400 per week, which was a lot during the Depression. She would travel the country in her white Cord automobile, once giving 23 talks in 25 days. She spent time on Purdue University's campus from 1935 to 1937 as a part-time career counselor for women. In fact, the silver, twin-engine Lockheed Electra that Earhart piloted on her last flight in 1937, an $80,000 "Flying Laboratory," was financed through the Purdue Research Foundation and private Purdue donors. Amelia helped organize the Women's 99 Group and became its first president. Later it would be called the Powder Puff Derby. Her philosophy was "He who tries and fails may, in himself, be a greater hero than the one for whom the band plays. Courage is the price that life exalts for granting peace. Please know that I'm quite aware of the hazards. I want to do it because I want to do it. Women must try to do things as men have tried. When they fail, their failure must be but a challenge to others."

CHAPTER 51

Founder/Boy Scouts

Robert Baden Powell

Lord Robert Baden Powell is best known for founding the International Boy Scout movement. His career as a military officer spreads 30 years as he rose to the rank of lieutenant general in the British Calvary.

Baden Powell (1857-1941) was the son of an Oxford University professor who died when Robert was 3 years old. Only an average student, Powell won a scholarship to Oxford. Determined to stay optimistic, he heard about an exam to qualify for an army commission. He finished fifth out of 718 in the test.

As a lieutenant, he was assigned to India in September 1876 with the 13th Hussars. He was determined to be a positive role model and sought out men to pattern his life after. He had the ability for bringing out the intelligence, initiative, and self-reliance of his men.

One of the worst enemies of troops overseas was boredom and low morale. He organized plays, painted scenery, and dressed up in costume and starred in his own productions. His philosophy was "You can capture more flies with honey than with vinegar."

In 1857, he was given command of the Fifth Dragon Guards. Noticing that the men were often sick with fever, he ordered them to stay out of a local bazaar. Their fevers cleared. He had amusement facilities built on base so they no longer had reason to go to the local bazaar.

In 1858, he served in Afghanistan. He saw that British troops lost the element of surprise because officers had to yell out orders to their men. Back in England, he thought about what would happen, and how to communicate orders with hand signals. The idea caught on and was adopted by other regiments.

From 1899 to 1902, he was involved in the Boer War. With just a small garrison, he withstood a much larger and better-armed force during a 217-day siege of Mafeking in Africa. It was considered a turning point of the war.

Returning to England in 1903, the effects of the war lingered on with a general depression of trade. Wages dropped, unemployment rose, children begged in the streets. 30 percent of the population suffered from malnutrition. Slums were more evident. Crime, drunkenness, and vandalism were prevalent. He witnessed the decrease in sports and a vast increase in "spectators" with mobs coming out simply to watch. His heart sickened seeing thousands of boys and young men pale, narrow-chested, and hunched up, numbers of them smoking and betting.

In April 1906, Baden Powell came up with a program called "Scouting for Boys," which incorporated many of the things he learned in the siege of Mafeking. Scouting for Boys incorporated the virtues of obedience and preparedness, devotion and duty, cheerfulness, helpfulness, and doing a good deed daily.

On the 29th of July 1907, Baden Powell took his young men to Browsee Island, which had 560 acres of thickly wooded land with two small lakes. The purpose of the camp was to learn to tie knots, learn to cook, tell stories and learn the principles of scouting. The 21 boys were divided into four patrols, each patrol having a name from the animal kingdom.

Baden Powell loved the outdoors. It is fitting that he said before he died, "The world has been awfully good to me. I have had a most extraordinary happy life." On January 8, 1941, the founder of the Boy Scouts passed away in Nyeri, Kenya.

CHAPTER 52

Salesman/Brushes

Alfred C. Fuller

Alfred C. Fuller (1885-1973) built a company that became known for its hardworking sales force. His Fuller Brush Company revolutionized the manufacturing process for brushes and made door-to-door selling acceptable.

The eleventh of 12 children, Fuller was born and reared in the farming community of Wellsford, Nova Scotia. As a child, he picked berries for one cent a quart. If he hustled, he could earn 30 cents over a 12-hour day. Determined to move up in the world, Fuller, then 18, moved to Boston in 1903.

Over the next 3 years he moved from job to job finally working for William Staples selling brushes door-to-door. Fuller saw the potential. He knew if he could demonstrate the brushes, instead of telling customers about them, he'd do well.

Many of the brushes were not made very well. He asked customers for suggestions on how they would change the brushes, what brushes they needed, and what they wanted a brush to do. Suggestions to Staples on design changes were ignored.

In 1906, he decided to form his own company. He sketched out his designs and with $375 bought the needed equipment to makes brushes. He wanted only the best quality brushes, and worked countless hours to meet high standards. Customers loved the new practical designs which sold well. In the first year he made $8,500.

The success of the business tired him out. There was no way he could keep up with the demand, it was time to delegate. In 1909, he placed an ad in *Everybody's* magazine appealing for salesmen. Thousands of responses came in, and Fuller hired 270 dealers across the U.S.

Soon the Fuller Brush man became a welcome caller to doorways everywhere in America. Fuller's success was built on his strong reliance on personal relationships. He kept his word, and he tried to be cheerful and fair. People wanted to work hard for him. He put people he trusted in business areas he couldn't directly oversee.

The company motto reads, "With equal opportunity to all, and due consideration for each person involved in every transaction, a business will succeed." By 1919, his business grew to $1 million per year. By 1960, sales totaled $109 million. Fuller never let success give him a swelled head. His strategy for success was staying humble. With no formal education, Fuller Brushmen had become an American institution.

CHAPTER 53

Entrepreneur/Chewing Gum

William Wrigley Jr.

William Wrigley Jr. was born in Philadelphia in 1861. His father was in the scouring soap business. Young Wrigley grew up working in his father's business. He traveled for 10 years on the road calling on both small as well as large merchants. His father wanted to remain small, but Wrigley had big dreams. Once he felt he had enough experience selling, he decided to move on.

Arriving in Chicago in 1891, he had just $32 in his pocket to get merchants to buy more of his soap; he'd throw in a free box of baking powder. Soon he discovered that the merchants were more interested in his baking powder, so he started selling baking powder and giving away free gum. When merchants started asking about the gum, he knew he had a winner.

Wrigley rented space and started his own firm making and selling gum. He knew that customers wanted good products and also discovered that people would feel good if they thought that they were getting more than they bargained for. He'd throw in freebies such as handbags, umbrellas, cash registers and cheese slicers with no strings attached. His strategy made a big impression.

In 1899, when six major chewing gum companies decided to merge, Wrigley decided not to join. It would be a challenge to compete against them. Trusting his own vision, he believed his gum was the best.

In 1907, a slump in the market caused businesses to cut their advertising budgets. The other gum companies cut back on their promotions. He felt that with everything else decreasing their marketing efforts, this was the right time to go full force. Twice before he had failed to penetrate the New York market and failed. This time he flooded the city with billboards and posters. Employees handed out free gum.

The campaign was so well received that he decided to expand to other cities. By 1910, Wrigley's Spearmint gum was America's favorite brand. Being an optimist, Wrigley said, "A man's doubts and his fears are his worst enemies." A slogan placed by his desk read, "Nothing great was ever achieved without enthusiasm."

Wrigley looked for ways to energize himself. He exercised everyday, long before it was fashionable. He felt his health and vigor was his greatest asset. If he didn't feel good, he figured the company wouldn't thrive.

Wrigley believed that if he treated his employees like winners, they would become winners. So in 1916, he purchased the Chicago Cubs baseball team. His players rode in the finest trains, wore the highest-quality uniforms, and stayed in the best hotels. If they saw themselves as elite, they would play on a higher level. The team was a fan favorite with frequent sellouts.

Even when he reached the top, there wasn't a job Wrigley wouldn't do. He packed, and sold, as the occasion demanded. No work was beneath him. Often he was found on the factory floor or in the stockroom. He died in 1932 in Phoenix, Arizona. Today, Wrigley is the leading producer of chewing gum in the world.

CHAPTER 54

Author/Western Novels

Louis L'Amour

Louis L'Amour (1908-88) was born in Jamestown, North Dakota. At age 15, he left home to find work. L'Amour made no effort to learn a trade; instead he had a multitude of different jobs over his lifetime. All he had to offer was his physical strength and the use of his two hands.

What were those jobs that would prepare him later in life to become such a prolific writer? Among them: living as a miner, a gold prospector, an elephant handler, a sailor, a fruit picker, a lumberjack, a professional boxer, a cattle skinner in Texas, a bailer of water out of ships bound for Asia, a tank officer during World War II, a sod carrier, a concrete mixer, a shoveler of sand and gravel, and a ditch digger.

L'Amour kept his eye on his real goal, which was to tell stories for his livelihood. His intention was to write, but he never thought of his day job to be a waste of time. He planned to make use of every single experience in his stories later. Rough times gave him all the grist for the mill, and he knew that someday this knowledge would be incorporated into his stories.

Finding time to write when he wasn't working proved challenging. He would write in ship quarters, bunkhouses, hotel rooms and local libraries. He would also write while sitting in hammocks. L'Amour believed that a writer cannot know too much. Sooner or later everything he does know will find its uses. "A writer's brain is like a magician's hat. If you're going to get anything out of it, you have to put something in first."

L'Amour published his first short story in 1935 and was paid $6.54 for it. He kept cranking out stories, one after another. When an editor turned him down, to combat discouragement, he was already working on the next story. To combat writer's block, he would start writing, no matter what, until ideas started flowing. "You can sit and look at a page for a long time and nothing will happen, start writing and it will."

Over the years, L'Amour was inspired to write 86 novels, 15 collections of short stories and two works of nonfiction. His books have sold 225 million copies around the world and have been translated into 20 languages. He was winner of the Congressional Gold Medal in 1982 and was awarded the Medal of Freedom by President Reagan in 1984.

L'Amour believed that people were interested in hearing about places beyond their reach. America's western frontier fit the bill. Reading old newspapers and diaries of old settlers and talking to old-timers gave him many ideas.

CHAPTER 55

Inventors/Tools

Black and Decker

Today we take for granted the personal power tool, such as the drill, power saw and other handheld tools. But it wasn't always that way. An industrial electric drill used to be a cumbersome piece of machinery. It weighed up to 50 pounds and required two men to operate, while a third controlled the power source.

S. Duncan Black (1883-1951) and Alonzo G. Decker (1884-1950) figured that there must be a better way. The two were trying to develop a portable version of the electric drill. One of them noticed a pistol that was lying nearby on a table. They figured they could adapt a power tool with a pistol grip and the on-off switch as the trigger. By the time they finished, the drill was easy to handle and allowed workers to be more accurate. As a result, Black and Decker launched the portable tools industry.

Black and Decker met while working at the Roland telegraph company. They decided to start their own company in 1910. Decker borrowed $1,200 from his father-in-law. Black sold his 1907 Maxwell, a car he loved. Black excelled in sales and Decker was more engineering oriented. Black and Decker shared power. They knew from past experiences that divided management could ruin a company. Employees called them "Black, the Boss," and "Decker, the Chief."

Both men had a mechanical flair from a young age. As a boy Decker rigged a hopper to feed his family's horses automatically by connecting it to an alarm clock. Later in New York he created a device that resulted in the first cab meter.

Black and Decker were innovative salesmen. To demonstrate their various machines to industrial workers, special buses built by Pierce-Arrow became "School Rooms on Wheels." By 1925, they had traveled all over the U.S. In 1929, they loaded their equipment onto six-passenger travel-air monoplanes and created flying showrooms. Even when the economy dipped in 1921, they continued to advertise while competitors cut back on marketing.

Black and Decker made their pitch to industry, not consumers. A washing machine flopped in 1930. A consumer drill failed because the price was too high. It took a son, Al Decker Jr. to get it right. He noticed that post-World War II power tools were so popular with defense plant workers that they were stealing them and taking them home. In 1946, Decker Jr. introduced a drill for $16.00. The strategy worked, and Black and Decker products quickly became a household name.

CHAPTER 56

Entrepreneur/Foods

H.J. Heinz

Henry John Heinz's (1844-1919) first attempt in business ended in bankruptcy. The banks pulled his credit as the result of a financial panic in 1875.

Although his business obligations were erased under the law, he believed that the foundation of business was integrity. It took him the next 9 years to pay off the creditors because Heinz felt it was his moral obligation.

Heinz wouldn't cut corners with other businesses, his customers or employees. "Honorable or not at all," he said when he had a chance to buy off some remaining creditors; it took five years for the bankruptcy to be discharged.

When Heinz was 31 years old, in 1875, he knew he had let investors down. Few of his friends stood by him. He resolved to start again. In 1876, with only $3,000, he started F & J Heinz Company with his cousin Frederick and his brother John as partners. To ensure success, he traveled from Pittsburgh to Philadelphia to re-open business ties. To save money, he sat up all night in the day coach. He also inspected his fields on foot rather than by horseback.

Heinz determined to be patient. He built the company step-by-step and wouldn't let the business grow too fast. By 1900,

Heinz was making more than 200 products. He was the largest producer of pickles, vinegar, and ketchup in the U.S. Employment had grown to 2,800 with factories in six states serving customers around the world.

His motto for success was "To do a common thing uncommonly well." While most food producers were ardent opponents of the 1906 Pure Food and Drug Act, Heinz supported it. He wouldn't shortchange customers knowing he was dependent on their goodwill. He also spent heavily to give away free samples at grocery stores, fairs, expositions and food shows.

Confident of the quality of his products, Heinz was among the first factory owners to invite the public to visit. By 1920, more than 20,000 people toured the Pittsburgh plant.

To avert labor trouble, he built an auditorium on company grounds and held concerts, dance recitals, Christmas parties and other activities. Women were offered free instruction in cooking, dressmaking, drawing, and other pursuits—even on becoming American citizens. Workers also could use the company pool or gymnasium. Receiving an award for his good treatment of workers, Heinz said his "primary motive was their welfare." But it wasn't bad for business either.

CHAPTER 57

Industrialist/U.S. Steel

Andrew Carnegie

Andrew Carnegie (1835-1919) was born in Dunfermline, Scotland. His father lost his job as a weaver when the looms were automated. Seeing very little opportunity in Scotland, the family moved to Pittsburgh in 1848.

At age 12, Carnegie had only five years of schooling when he went to work in a textile mill as a bobbin boy. Later he found work tending a steam engine and boiler. He believed in doing more than was asked of him.

In 1849, Carnegie joined Western Union. In 1853, he took a position as personal telegrapher and assistant to Thomas Scott, an executive with the Pennsylvania railroad. Studying the railroads operations, he was able to suggest innovations. One suggestion was to burn railroad cars after accidents rather than try to remove them. This cleared the tracks more quickly. In 1859, he became superintendent of the western division of the railroad. Carnegie was always careful with his money. He said, "Take care of the pennies and the pounds will take care of themselves." Even when he earned $2 or $3 a week, he'd put a little aside. In 1856, he had invested his savings, plus a small loan, in the Woodruff Sleeping Car Company. Soon his investment was returning $5,000 a year, which was double his railroad salary.

After several more successful investments, he was in on the first major oil strike in Titusville, Pennsylvania. Carnegie wanted to have his own company and organized Keystone Bridge Company with the idea to replace wooden bridges with iron. In 1872, he saw Henry Bessemer's blast furnaces in England. He saw the possibilities of steel with its strength and flexibility.

Returning to Pittsburgh, he planned his first steel mill. Deploying a clever marketing strategy, he named his plant the Edgar Thomson Works, after the president of the Pennsylvania railroad. His first order for 2,000 steel rails came from the railroad.

Carnegie admitted his limitations and hired a chemist to improve his furnaces. He hired top accountants to initiate cost accounting measures. As a result, he was able to reduce the cost of rails from $160 a ton in 1875 to $17 a ton by 1890. He believed in making a higher-quality product than the purchaser required.

Often Carnegie would take up to six months traveling. He did not want his mind to get itself into a rut. During panics or depressions when stock prices fell, he would put every penny into building up his facilities. He only invested in collateral businesses like coal, coal mines and raw materials for his plants. His advice was "put your eggs in one basket and watch the basket." This is the way to make money.

In 1901, J.P. Morgan bought Carnegie Steel and merged it to become U.S. Steel; the purchase price was $480 million. Carnegie gave most of his money away. He founded Carnegie Institutions, which funded colleges, universities, public libraries, and he donated nearly 8,000 pipe organs to churches. He believed the wealthy had a moral obligation to act as stewards for society. He said, "The man who dies rich dies disgraced." By the time of his death, he had given over 90 percent of his money away.

CHAPTER 58

Patriot/Constitution

James Madison

James Madison (1751-1836) served as the fourth President of the United States and was known as the Father of the Constitution. Madison was a well-educated person who learned reading, writing and arithmetic at home until age 11. His parents then sent him to boarding school where he spent five years learning Latin, Greek, French, Italian, algebra, geometry, and geography.

Madison was a voracious reader. He spent two years studying under the Reverend Thomas Martin to prepare for college. Once at the College of New Jersey at Princeton, he sought out college president John Witherspoon as a mentor who later would be one of the signers of the Declaration of Independence. Madison finished three years of study in two, in 1771.

History and politics inspired him, losing his first election to Virginia's House of Delegates, he went on to win other posts and later to the Continental Congress. Shy by nature, he worked to overcome it by being absolutely sure of his subject. He would study the issue at hand and all the surrounding arguments and would be the most well-prepared member of his session. Madison knew the virtue of diligence and hard work. He served in the Continental Congress for nearly four years. It is believed by many that without him, the Constitution wouldn't have been written.

Madison read every book and pamphlet on the problems of Confederacies and Republican Government. He took a lot of notes and kept his findings in a pocket-size booklet to refer to in debates. Many of those notes found their way into the "Federalist Papers" which argued for ratifying the Constitution.

On May 3, 1878, he arrived in Philadelphia early so he could talk to all the delegates before the convention began. His research produced the so-called Virginia Plan, which became the framework for the Constitution. In it, he outlined the checks-and-balances system that created a central government and preserved individual liberty.

Madison knew the task before him, yet his preparation and precise attention to detail paid off. He spoke 161 times, more than any other delegate, on every subject under consideration. After the convention endorsed the Constitution, he wrote 24 of the 85 Federalist Papers and co-authored another three with Alexander Hamilton. He also served in the first Congress to help get the Bill of Rights passed. He went on to serve as president from 1809 to 1816.

Madison believed in individual liberty and pursued the goal of an independent and democratic America. His was a lifelong devotion to learning and preparation.

CHAPTER 59

Inventor/Farming Implements

John Deere

In the early 1800s, blacksmiths produced many of the horseshoes and farm implements for farmers. John Deere (1804-86) was a master blacksmith, a trade he developed through years of work in his native Vermont. He was noted for his highly polished hay forks and shovels, and they were in high demand until Vermont's economy faltered in the mid-1830s.

Like many of his neighbors, Deere looked for new opportunities elsewhere. He realized that the frontier of America's prairies needed his services. He headed west with tools and a small amount of cash. Grand Detour, Illinois, was such a place, and he wasted no time in getting to work. Within two days, his forge was running and customers were coming into his shop.

The pioneer farmer's equipment did not work well in the prairie soil. In New England, where soil is sandy, plowing is easier. Prairie soil, in contrast, stuck to plow bottoms. Farmers called it "gumbo" because it's so thick. Farmers had to stop often to scrape the gumbo off their plows. Deere heard about the problem in 1837 and saw what the prairie soil did to farmer's plows. Studying the problem, he decided to apply a highly polished cast-steel surface. Taking a large broken saw blade, he fastened the blade to a plow moldboard and gave it a try. It cut through the gumbo and did what earlier plows couldn't do—keep the soil off the plow itself. This breakthrough opened up more land to cultivation.

Deere was up against the traditional practice under which blacksmith's built to customers orders. To grab farmer's interest, he hired agents to take plows door-to-door and actually demonstrate them. The demonstrations were a huge success.

To keep up with demand, Deere ordered special raised steel from England. To get it to Grand Detour, it traveled across the sea, up the Mississippi River, then 40 miles by wagon. Looking for a better way, he learned of a new raised-steel plant opening in Pittsburgh. He decided to move his factory to Moraine, Illinois, which was right on the Mississippi River.

Ten years after making his first plow, he was making 1,000 plows a year. His mission statement "Always stick to high quality" would steer Deere and Company to become one of the world's dominant manufacturers of farm equipment. "I will never put my name on a plow that does not have in it the best that is in me," Deere said. "If we don't improve our product, somebody else will."

CHAPTER 60

Entrepreneur/Pepperidge Farms

Margaret Rudkin

Margaret Rudkin (1897-1967), founder of Pepperidge Farm Co., was born in New York City. Married to a wealthy stockbroker, she lived on a large estate in Fairfield, Conn. She had every material thing she could want, but when one of her children was diagnosed with asthma, in 1935, she looked for a way to help him find relief. A physician suggested a diet of wholesome food might improve her son's condition. She checked old family cookbooks and started baking even though she had never baked a loaf of bread in her life.

Her first efforts failed, but she kept trying until she created a bread that was not only healthful, but delicious as well. At first, Rudkin baked breads for her family alone. Then the doctor asked her to make bread for him and his patients. Seeing how much people liked her breads, Rudkin decided to expand. Next was a mail-order business from home.

In 1937, she decided to approach a local grocer. The move took courage, at age 40 she made her first sales call. It was a time when women did not go into business. It was also when the nation was in a depression, so the chips were stacked against new businesses succeeding—even more daunting, she sold her bread for 25 cents a loaf, when most sold for about a dime.

Her method for selling was to give the store manager and clerks samples. After they tasted her bread, Rudkin would give a sales pitch about the healthful ingredients she used and would leave a few loaves behind. The method worked by the time she got home. After her first sales effort, the grocer called and asked for more. He'd already sold the bread she had left him.

As volume grew and her kitchen became too small, Rudkin took over an empty stable on her farm. The company continued to grow. When shortages of some ingredients were not available during World War II, she refused to compromise quality. She discontinued products rather than use inferior ingredients.

She was quick to recognize opportunity. Touring Europe in 1948, she discovered a selection of delicious cookies. Rather than guess at the ingredients, she contracted with a Belgian bakery to supply a new line of cookies for Pepperidge Farm. To give them an international cachet, she named them after cities and resorts in Europe: Milano, Brussels and Bordeaux. They were introduced to the U.S. in 1956 and are popular products today.

When a new product was introduced, she insisted on taking the first bite. After World War II, she went to independent distributors rather than having her own trucks. The *New Yorker* magazine joked that she produced a product 99.9 percent of the public didn't want. "I'm only trying to please a minority who want a good loaf of bread and are willing to pay for it," she said.

In a speech in 1962, Rudkin said, "The IBM company uses that wonderful one-word slogan, 'Think,' but I believe we should add another word to it, and that word is 'try.' There is no use thinking if you don't carry out your ideas. Go ahead and try to do something a little better than it has ever been done before."

CHAPTER 61

Inventor/Telegraph

Samuel F.B. Morse

In 1835, Samuel F.B. Morse was nearly broke. As an art professor at New York University, he struggled just to buy food, but Morris had a great interest in electricity. When he wasn't teaching or printing a portrait, he was devoting his time to making a model of a telegraph. He used a handmade battery and an old artist's canvas stretcher to hold the model together. Too poor to buy insulated wire, he bought cheap wire in pieces and soldered them together. Wrapping the wire bit by bit with cotton thread, he relied on old clock parts to move a paper tape across the frame where messages were to be recorded. He then used a swinging lever to support a recording pencil and pole piece of an electromagnet. As the electromagnet activated the swinging lever, the pencil traced a wavy line on the paper tape that corresponded to the received signal pulses.

To send the pulses, Morse developed a tapping system, a combination of short interruptions (dots) and long interruptions (dashes) stood for each letter of the alphabet. It became known as the Morse Code.

Prior to his teaching at New York University, Morse was a student at Yale from 1805 to 1810. He took classes in physics, astronomy and chemistry where he learned about electricity. He spent hours constructing models of Alessandro Volta and William Cruikshanks batteries. One question loomed in his mind: Could electricity pass instantly through a long wire? His answer came in 1832. On a voyage from France to New York, he met Charles Jackson, an expert on electricity, who assured him that it would pass through any length of wire. Morse failed in his first try to make his machine work on 40 feet of wire. To solve the problem, he went from using one battery to 20. In 1837, he succeeded in sending codes for over 10 miles.

Morse couldn't market the invention without funding. Approaching government officials in 1837, he was turned down. After lobbying Congress three more times, they appropriated $30,000 for a 40-mile line between Washington, D.C. and Baltimore. After the line was completed on May 24, 1844, he transmitted the following words to Baltimore: "What hath God wrought?" Morse never lost faith in the practicality of the invention.

CHAPTER 62

Resolve/Footwear

Dr. William Scholl

D r. William Scholl (1882-1968) grew up on a farm in LaPorte, Indiana. When his work for the day was done, he'd go to his grandfather's bench where he learned how to make shoes. A perfectionist, Scholl tried to make shoes that were comfortable. But as soon as family members finished working, they'd put on slippers. It seemed no matter how well he shaped leather and sole, the shoes weren't comfortable. He resolved to find a way to make shoes people wanted to wear. At age 16, he traveled to Michigan City, Indiana, and signed on as an apprentice at a shoemaker's shop. Although he knew the basics of cobbling, he started out at the bottom, sweeping floors and pulling old heels off boots to be repaired.

At 18, Scholl went to Chicago and got a job as a shoe clerk at Ruppert's shoe store. Working long hours, he looked for ways to make shoes comfortable. No matter how the shoes were sized, people's feet still hurt. He decided the problem wasn't the shoes, it was the feet that wore them. While still working in the shoe store, he enrolled at Illinois Medical College. Scholl learned and memorized every bone, tendon and muscle. Soon he realized that people's feet hurt because of their shape.

If the arch wasn't high enough, the foot collapsed on itself. He zeroed in on the arch as the problem. Putting together leather, steel and a spring, he came up with the first arch support. Patients and customers were thrilled. Scholl knew he had a best-seller. Listening to customers, he hit upon a name when one man said, "That gadget of yours is a real foot-easer."

To get the word out, Scholl took the direct approach, pounding the pavement from shoe store to shoe store in Chicago. Whenever he approached a shop owner, Scholl would say "Give me five minutes of your time, and I will show you how to satisfy your customers so well that they will be your customers for life." To see him as an authority, he dressed to appear older, wearing stiff collars and a cutaway coat that was customary attire for physicians.

In 1904, he founded the Scholl Manufacturing Company in Chicago. To keep himself motivated, he came up with a motto: "Early to bed, early to rise, work like hell and advertise." Scholl's budget was small at first, yet he wanted broad coverage and avoided large ads in one or two newspapers. Instead, he designed a series of 1-inch ads that ran all over the country.

In 1904, he received his medical degree and changed the name of his company to Dr. Scholl Inc. In his factories, Scholl hung signs that said "Quality, if it isn't right it's wrong—No halfway measure can ever be right." In 1962, *Time Magazine* praised Scholl as the "Man who made the world foot conscious."

CHAPTER 63

Dedication/American Red Cross

Clara Barton

Clarissa "Clara" Barton (1821-1912) grew up on a farm in Oxford, Mass. She was a shy person as a young girl. Her pets, which included a cat, dog, rooster and colt, followed her around. Her soothing, gentle voice calmed the pets, even her snapping turtle and turkey let her pet them.

One day her brother's hunting dog got his paw run over by a wagon. The dog was lying in the barn, whimpering in pain and wouldn't let anyone touch the injured paw. Barton was sure she could help, even though her family was afraid he would bite her out of pain. Speaking softly to the dog, then gently touching his paw, she washed, treated and wrapped the paw with a bandage. When she was done, the dog gratefully licked her hand.

The family soon found that she had a way with sick people, too. Her brother fell, hit his head and was laid up with a fever. Though her brother's illness lasted a long time, she patiently helped nurse him back to health. While in high school, smallpox spread through the neighborhood. She helped nurse and tend to other's needs. When the threat of disease was over, the neighborhood gave her a new leather saddle to show their gratitude.

Spending a few years as a teacher and copyist in the Patent Office in Washington, D.C., she did not seem satisfied. When a trainload of wounded soldiers arrived in the city, Barton decided to get involved. It was 1861, the Civil War was underway, and she was appalled at the lack of supplies and care for the injured soldiers, leading many of the injured soldiers to her sister's house to treat their wounds.

Soon overcrowded camps and lack of hygiene, staff, and supplies took their toll. Diseases spread rapidly. Within two months, 30 percent of the army was sick or wounded. The hospitals were overflowing. She became a one-woman relief agency, cooking food and buying food out of her own salary. As word spread in her hometown of Massachusetts, women started sending her boxes of food and medical supplies. The supplies kept coming until she had to rent three warehouses to store the boxes.

Barton wanted to nurse the soldiers herself. Army officials resisted and didn't want female nurses at first. They told her their soldiers didn't need any help, but she knew better. So Barton sought out influential people who won her permission to nurse the soldiers. Soon she was slogging through mud and filth in the battlefields, to reach those who needed help. While drumming up supplies— or later support for the Red Cross—Barton strived to be friendly. She worded her requests carefully, so as not to seem pushy. As a result, many felt they'd known her for a long time, even if they'd just met her. Her smile, sparkle in her dark brown eyes, and a relaxed informality drew people to her. Later she founded the American Red Cross.

CHAPTER 64

Discipline/Boxing

Joe Lewis

Joe Lewis (1914-1981) was born in Lafayette, Alabama. When Joe was 2, his father was hospitalized for mental illness, leaving Joe's mother to care for eight children in a run-down house. In 1924, his mother remarried, and the family moved to Detroit. While at a trade show, Lewis discovered boxing. Working at a truck factory during the day, he trained at night and on weekends. After several years of training in the ring, he turned professional boxer in 1934. He took on tough opponents, beating them all. By searching out their weak spots, then hitting them as hard and as often as he could, he memorized different punches, training his mind as rigorously as his body.

Lewis's career was managed by John Roxborough, who set down stiff rules: a strict diet, rigorous training, and no easy fights. Night clubs were out. Lewis didn't smoke or drink. He would wake up each day at 6:00 A.M. and run six miles.

He asked John Roxborough to manage him. Roxborough enlisted Jack Blackburn to train Lewis. Punching away on a heavy bag, his punches grew more powerful, but power itself didn't win matches. By sparring with lighter, quicker boxers, Lewis had to speed his own pace to match theirs. As a result, Lewis's power and agility devastated opponents.

156

Being black, Lewis was told that he would never win the championship by merely outscoring white opponents. Blackburn told him "you gotta knock them out to get anywhere." His reputation as a tough fighter soon put him in New York. In his first fight in the Big Apple, Louis destroyed former heavyweight champ Primo Carnera.

By 1937, Lewis was ready for his first title fight. Keeping a strict schedule, he rose at 5:00 A.M. and ran 10 miles. Then back to bed until breakfast at 10.00 A.M. Sweets, which he loved, had no place in his diet. All his preparation worked. Louis knocked out James Braddock, the champ, in the eighth round to win the title.

Lewis's road to the title had some bumps. Before beating Braddock, he lost to German fighter Max Schmeling in 1936. He vowed that he wouldn't answer to the title of champ until he beat Schmeling in a rematch. The rematch came in 1938. Louis didn't repeat the mistakes he made in the first fight. He trained harder than ever. With Blackburn, he watched films of the first bout. Louis was so focused that his "mental attitude is the best I've ever known him to attain," said Roxborough.

The dedication paid off. Lewis knocked out Schmeling in the first round at Yankee Stadium. He went on to defend the heavyweight title in 25 bouts, more time than any other champion. His willingness to take on all challengers defined his greatness. Lewis retired undefeated in 1949, the longest reign in the title's history.

CHAPTER 65

Innovator/Toy Trains

Joshua Lionel Cowen

Joshua Lionel Cowen (1877-1965) was born in New York to immigrant parents from Eastern Europe. An inventor and tinkerer, he once cracked open his sister's bisque doll head to see how the eyes moved. As a youth, he claimed to have invented the first battery-powered doorbell.

Despite an interest in science, Cowen was often truant from school. Cowen had no interest in college. He wanted to be an inventor. In 1898, he worked at ACME Electric Lamp Company, where he patented a fuse for igniting photographer's flash powder. The U.S. Navy found the fuse was useful to explode mines and paid him $12,000 for the use of it.

As a youth he had grown up near the lines of railroads. Toy trains weren't exciting and had to be pushed by hand or wound up. He built his own battery-operated, chugging toy train that didn't need pushing or rewinding.

In September of 1900, Cowen opened up Lionel Manufacturing Co., producing and selling electric novelties and low-voltage motors. By that time, the toy electric train had become popular. By late 1901, Lionel Manufacturing began producing trains exclusively. He introduced transformers for use with electric house current in 1906. To get the kids more interested in trains, he introduced interactive accessories so children could use their imagination.

Cowen wanted Lionel trains to look and move like real ones, so he made replicas such as Baltimore and Ohio's new electric locomotive. Cowen knew how to promote. He kept track of who bought his trains so he could tailor new models to their tastes. On Father's Day in 1946, he opened his showroom in New York to dads only. To get in, men had to provide proof that they were fathers.

Once, a customer complained that Lionel's toy signals should be black and white—as they were in reality—instead of the bright colors Lionel sold. Cowen replied "Do you know who actually buys toy trains and accessories? It's the women—mothers, sisters and the aunts of the kids who play with them. Don't forget, women buy on color and want it bright looking."

Nearly 100 years later, Lionel LLC based in Chesterfield, Michigan, remains the leading manufacturer and marketer of model toy trains. In 1998, the U.S. Postal Service honored him with a commemorative stamp.

His philosophy was to cater to the masses rather than the classes if you want to get the most out of any article sold to the public.

CHAPTER 66

Determination/Football

Walter Payton

Walter Payton was born in Columbia, Mississippi, in 1954. His devout Baptist parents didn't want him to play football like his elder brother Eddie. When Walter reached high school, he didn't start playing football until his junior year.

The first time he carried the ball, he ran 60 yards for a touchdown. Payton realized that ability alone would not carry him to the top. He had to work hard. To train, he found a hill on a levee of the Pearl River. He built a 65-yard course, pushing himself to develop his stamina and his leg strength. In addition to the hill, he lifted weights regularly.

Entering nearby Jackson State University, he set several college records, including the all-time college scoring mark. He graduated with a B.A. in 1975. The Chicago Bears chose him as their first-round draft pick after graduating. It was said that Payton could lift a 100-pound dumbbell with one hand. Even though the Bears were a mediocre team, much of his career he kept improving. His drive to excel kept his focus on always improving.

On the field, Payton was rarely satisfied. He didn't run out of bounds at the end of a play, preferring instead to finish the opponent. Payton said, "It's not a matter of pride, it's a matter of survival, because if you let those guys beat up on you, you won't be in there too long." To him, succeeding depended on more than physical toughness. "I wasn't the biggest or the fastest or the strongest, but I was the smartest." Payton stood 5'10" and weighted 205 pounds.

To stay healthy, he reasoned that most leg injuries came from being hit when the leg is bent too much. So he developed a more straight-legged style, trying never to let his knees bend more than 30 degrees. Other running backs averaged closer to 90 degrees. His reasoning paid off, he only missed one game in his pro career.

Criticism spurred him on. If he heard fans say he wouldn't do anything today, he would really become determined. On a lighter side, he kept teammates loose with his antics of walking 50 yards on the sidelines on his hands. His attitude helped pull the team together. In 1985, the Bears won the Super Bowl XX.

Payton holds NFL records for the most yards rushing (16,726), most rushing attempts (3,338), most rushing yards in a game (235), most total career yardage (21,803), most rushing touchdowns (110), and most games rushing for 100 yards or more (77). He went to the Pro Bowl nine times and was named NFL player of the year 1977 and 1985. He was elected to the Pro Football Hall of Fame in 1993.

Even as he faced death from cancer from a rare liver disease, he stayed positive. He didn't ask "Why Me?" said his teammate Mike Singletary who visited him the day before he died in 1999.

CHAPTER 67

Pioneer/Watches

Joseph Bulova

Joseph Bulova (1851-1935) was born in Austria-Hungary and moved to the U.S. As a young adult, he learned the tradition of Old World craftsmanship that demanded every watch or piece of jewelry be a piece of art. But he also realized that mass production and interchangeable parts could revolutionize watchmaking.

Setting up a small family jewelry shop in New York City, he learned that the military had stopped using pocket watches and hand watches and had switched to wearing wristwatches. They were simple timepieces latched to leather straps. Bulova and his son, Arde, experimented by adding fine Swiss watch movements and decorative designs. In 1919, Bulova introduced the first full line of wristwatches with jeweled works. Sales took off.

Up to this time, the earliest wristwatches were small clocks that dangled from women's bracelets. They were perceived as feminine ornaments, and men didn't wear wristwatches because they were considered effeminate. He bet that wristwatches would be a hit with men. In the 1920s, sales rocketed. In 1924, Bulova introduced the first line of women's wristwatches which were trim. Some had diamond accents.

Bulova believed in standardizing every part of his watchmaking. Each part was made to a ten-thousandth of an inch and was interchangeable with any other Bulova watch. Before this time, replacement parts had to be duplicated by hand which could take a long time.

To advertise his company, B.U.L.O.V.A., Bulova and his son, Arde, produced a radio commercial with the famous slogan, "At the tone, it's 8:00 P.M. Bulova watch time." It stuck in the minds of listeners and was used for years. Bulova watches became a household name. In 1927, 5000 special watches were made to commemorate Charles Lindbergh's first transatlantic flight.

Bulova knew how to plan for the unexpected. He was aware of wars and political upheavals that shook Europe. By 1929, he dismantled and shipped an entire Swiss watch factory to the U.S. He started hiring Swiss watch executives and resettled them in the U.S. Between 1930 and 1940, Bulova amassed plants and experts to manufacture complete watches without foreign parts or help.

In 1929, he patented a new type of clock for use in cars. By 1931, he began making some of the world's first electric clocks, which included wall and mantel clocks. By that time, Bulova had cornered about 50 percent of the U.S. market. Later, his commemorative watches honored the first Apollo moon astronauts and a host of other events in U.S. history.

CHAPTER 68

Inventor/International Harvester

Cyrus McCormick

Growing up on a farm in the hills of western Virginia, Cyrus McCormick watched in vain, for 15 years, as his father tried to invent a mechanical wheat harvester. His father's work on the harvester fascinated McCormick.

When his father finally gave up on the reaper, young Cyrus asked if he could take over. His father urged against it, stating it was a lost cause. McCormick was optimistic that he could make a successful reaper. In his mind, he'd already come up with a completely new design.

After two months, he had welded together a new machine which cut wheat at the rate of an acre per hour. This was considered an improvement over what a person could do with a scythe—a half acre in a day. He invited farmers to come and watch his machine in action. They were not impressed saying, "It's a wonderful contraption for stunts, but I'm running a farm, not a circus." Their skepticism was reinforced when the machine had a tendency to jam in wet weather or on hillsides.

McCormick thought that if he could get leading farmers to use the reaper, they'd be able to persuade others. But none of them felt comfortable using his reaper and didn't trust it. He was getting nowhere. Stumped, McCormick decided to quit making reapers for the next five years. He continued working at his iron business, but the reaper never left his thoughts, and he thought of ways to improve the reaper. Each year, he'd harvest the wheat on his father's 50-acre farm searching for ways to make his machine more reliable and efficient.

In 1841, McCormick redesigned the blade on his reaper so that the serrations went in two directions instead of one. The result was a dual cutting action. Suddenly, his machine chopped off wheat cleanly. Now, he was ready to market his invention again. In 1842, he sold just seven reapers.

Soon there were copycats. In 1843, a rival reaper, Obed Hussey, challenged him to a duel—they'd go head-to-head in a field to see who could harvest the most wheat. McCormick saw this as an opportunity to improve his design once and for all. Unfortunately for Hussey, it rained, and his machine jammed, lurched and couldn't cut through wet grain. McCormick's machine hummed along effortlessly. That year he sold 29 machines.

In 1848, McCormick moved his factory to Chicago from Virginia. By 1850, he was selling 1,500 reapers per year. Then in 1891, the Chicago fire destroyed his plant. McCormick saw this as an opportunity to expand outside the city.

In 1878, McCormick was elected to the French Academy of Science for increasing food and production in the U.S. and around the world. His manufacturing firm became International Harvester in 1902.

CHAPTER 69

Visionary/Piper Aircraft

William Piper

William Piper had a dream. He believed that airplanes would become as common as automobiles. They would be easy to buy and easy to fly. Although his dream did not grow as much as he intended, he gave birth to a generation of aircrafts that would make his name synonymous with light planes.

Born in 1881, at Knapps Creek, New York, Piper served in the Spanish-American War, earned an engineering degree from Harvard in 1903, and worked as a construction engineer. Piper bought $400 of stock in a failing airplane maker, The Taylor Co., which had recently moved to Bradford, Pennsylvania. Piper lived in Bradford and operated several successful oil wells there. He bought the stock to encourage industry in the town.

Two years later, he bought the concern's assets at a bankruptcy sale in 1931. Not knowing how to make planes, he kept C.G. Taylor as company president and chief engineer. Piper named himself treasurer. To keep Taylor motivated and the company growing, Piper gave him a half interest.

Piper produced the first Cub, a low-price plane in 1931. The company lost money up until 1935. This was the time of the Great Depression. Piper decided to offer a cheaper plane. Taylor objected, as he wanted to build a bigger, more expensive aircraft.

In 1936, Piper bought out Taylor and renamed it Piper Aircraft. The improved version caused sales to double in 1936, and the company earned its first profit.

To become more efficient, he instituted assembly-line technologies. Piper saw that all model T Fords were black. To encourage the same brand recognition, Piper used a yellow scheme for all Piper Cubs. Planes required more handwork than automobiles to make, so he had to hire more employees. To cut costs, all workers could take flying lessons for the cost of oil and gas, about $1 per hour. By 1940, Piper had 1,000 employees. The average age was 23 and they were paid 40 cents per hour. The auto industry was paying 90 cents per hour. The smart, eager boys were crazy about flying and were willing to work for nothing so that they could fly.

Just before the U.S. was plunged into war in 1941, military leaders wanted Piper to subcontract work from big airplane makers. Piper believed that the light planes were the best way to train pilots to fly. He gave the army 12 Piper Cubs. At first, the lightweight planes were scorned by military officers. But Piper's strategy was on the mark-training exercises showed that the small Cubs could be used for pilot training and artillery observations. By the end of the war, Piper had supplied the military with 7,000 planes. His Cubs served as the training craft for four out of five World War II pilots.

Cubs were used to carry plasma, supplies, and mail into thick jungles that were inaccessible to faster or larger planes. German fighter pilots earned twice as many points toward air medals for shooting down a Piper Cub. Few were shot down, because they were so maneuverable. Pilots would dive to the ground and duck around barns to escape enemy fire.

Piper helped his company produce more planes during his lifetime than any other manufacturer. Piper died in Lock Haven, Pennsylvania., in 1970. Today Piper Aircraft still produces seven different models.

CHAPTER 70

Manufacturer/Motor Vehicles

Soichiro Honda

Soichiro Honda (1906-1991) was born in Tenryo City, Japan. Honda was fascinated with motors. In his early years, he worked as an automobile mechanic. After years of learning how things worked, he decided it was better to create than repair. Striking out on his own, he opened several engine-related businesses, eventually founding Honda Motor Co. in 1948, in Hamamatsu, Japan, a motorbike manufacturer.

In 1954, Honda wanted to inspire his employees to produce the best motorcycles they could, so he wrote a letter to the employees stating that Honda Motor would develop a motorcycle that would win the Tourist Trophy Race. Held annually on the Isle of Man in the Irish Sea off mainland Britain, the event was one of the most prestigious motorcycle races in the world.

Honda went to see the Tourist Trophy Race and was awed at the level of competition. He questioned in his mind whether he could come up with the technology to win the race. He studied the competition, visiting the top motorcycle makers in Europe. Buying key engine parts, he took them back to Japan and examined them thoroughly. In 1961, he won the Tourist Trophy Race, the Italian Grand Prix and the Japanese title, becoming the first to win all three titles in a year.

Honda believed there was no substitute for excellent quality. He did not believe in protectionism. He felt developing better products was the answer. He believed that high-quality goods knew no boundaries. An American sales agent told Honda that his target of 7,500 motorcycles a month was "preposterous." The Honda Super Cub was introduced in 1958. It was light, small, and easy to ride. The company's slogan "You meet the nicest people on a Honda" was a hit with many Americans who were looking for a secondary, leisure vehicle. By 1968, Honda sold its millionth motorcycle in the U.S. By 1973, Honda owned 46 percent of the U.S. market.

Honda began producing cars in 1967. He was committed to reducing pollution and was the first to tackle the problem. He studied U.S. factory management and emulated "the rules of capitalism." He reminded his engineers of the goal to be number one in the world. He wasn't afraid of failure and believed success can only be achieved through repeated failure.

Honda's principles were part of his business philosophy. He believed that business without a philosophy may succeed at first but will eventually encounter opposition. An enterprise without moral principle, without a philosophy, and without willingness to serve the people cannot succeed.

CHAPTER 71

Manufacturer/Camping Gear

William Coleman

To pay for law school, William Coleman, (1870-1957) traveled around the country selling typewriters. One cold, rainy night in Brockton, Alabama, in 1899, he noticed an exceptionally bright light shining through the gloom from a lamp hanging from a drug store. It was the first lamp he'd found that was bright enough for him to read at night.

Coleman found the lamps distributor and landed a sales job. After a week, he'd sold only two lamps. The reason was a previous salesman had sold gasoline lamps that quit working after one month.

Coleman studied the situation and came to the realization that he was selling superior light, not lamps. Changing his strategy, Coleman offered to rent lamps to the merchants. Coleman told the merchants, "The other stores are going to be lighted by our service and you can't afford to go on selling in the dark."

Additionally, he gave them a contract to guarantee the service. Soon 100 merchants were signed up and service was extended to 20 towns.

To keep the market cornered, Coleman bought the patents for the lamps and the existing inventory. Two key principles guided his philosophy: First, "Whatever one manufactures or attempts to sell, must be the best of its kind." Second: "Nothing is ever sold until it adequately performs the purpose for which it was intended and gives value received to the consumer."

As electricity use expanded, he focused on rural farming markets. People raved about the lamp's convenience. He continued to innovate and started manufacturing gasoline stoves. When the army needed a compact stove for GI's during World War II, they insisted on the following specifications: The stove couldn't be bigger than a quart of milk; it must operate in temperatures minus 60 degrees below zero to 125 degrees above, and production must begin in two months.

Working seven days a week around the clock, the final product was delivered on time. It weighed 3 ½ pounds and met all the army's specifications. Famed war correspondent Ernie Pyle rated the Coleman "GI Pocket Stove" and the Jeep as the two most important pieces of non-combat equipment to come out of World War II. More than one million stoves were provided.

Over time, Coleman was recognized as an inventor, industrialist, entrepreneur and philanthropist, but he always referred to himself first as a salesman. He felt salesmen were key factors in bringing better things to more people. He believed in the joy of achievement and the principle of not letting money dominate a man. When a competitor's plant was wrecked by strikers, Coleman offered his plant's facilities. A compassionate man, whenever a flood or tornado or other natural disasters struck, he would provide free lanterns. He believed in public service, serving as a mayor of Wichita, Kansas, from 1923 to 1924.

CHAPTER 72

Passion/Wal-Mart

Samuel Moore Walton

Samuel Moore Walton was born in King Fisher, Oklahoma, in1918, and lived there until age 5. His family moved to Springfield, Marshall, Shelbina and Columbia, Missouri, in the next years of his young life. As a youth, Walton was ambitious. At school in Marshall, he bet other scouts that he would be first to make the rank of Eagle Scout. At age 13, he became the youngest Eagle Scout in Missouri at the time. Because of this training, he rescued a friend, Donald Peterson, from drowning.

From his time as a kid, he excelled at anything he set his mind to. A newspaper had a contest to see who could sell the most newspapers. He won the contest selling subscriptions door-to-door. Although he wasn't a gifted student, he did make it to the honor roll in high school. With him as a guard on the basketball team and quarterback on the football team, Hickman High School won State Championships.

Upon graduation from the University of Missouri in June 1940, Walton took a job with J.C. Penney. As a manager trainee, he made $75 a week. He loved retail from the beginning. Except for a little time out as an army officer, he would be in retail for the next fifty-plus years. After 18 months, he quit Penney and went to Prior, Oklahoma, to work for DuPont in a gun powder plant. At a bowling alley, he met Helen Robson, who would become his wife on February 14, 1943.

After the war, Walton ended up in Newport, Arkansas, as the owner of a money-losing Ben Franklin store. In September 1, 1945, the store was doing $72,000 per year, while the competitor across the street was doing $150,000 per year. Franklin had a very rigid system of doing business. Walton found ways to buy direct and save money. This drove Franklin crazy as he was supposed to buy at least 80 percent from them. After 2 ½ years, Walton had paid back his loan and turned the store into the top performer in the district. After five years, the little Ben Franklin store was doing $250,000 per year.

Seeing Walton's success, the landlord refused to renew the lease. He wanted to have his son run it. From that point on, Walton vowed he would read his leases more carefully. He sold out. At age 32, he found a store in Bentonville, Arkansas. He expanded it to 4,000 square feet and instituted self-service—a broad new concept. By 1952, he expanded to Fayetteville. His stores went by the name, "Walton's Five and Dime."

In the early days, variety store chains did not cross state borders. Hearing about a new shopping center in Ruskin Heights, part of Kansas City, it became the biggest store. In 1962, Walton changed the name of his stores to Wal-Mart. He liked that name because it only had seven letters and would save him money on signs.

On March 17, 1992, President Bush presented Sam Walton with the Presidential Medal of Freedom. Three weeks later, on Sunday, April 5, 1992, he died from a form of bone cancer. As of April 2002, a Wal-Mart and Sam's Clubs have over 500 stores and sales of $219 billion. Never letting success go to his head, he drove an old pickup truck. Tom Peters said, with the exception of Henry Ford, Sam Walton is the entrepreneur of the century.

CHAPTER 73

Determination/Author

Boris Pasternak

As a child, Boris Pasternak (1890-1960) started playing the piano at age 5. His family and friends were convinced that music was his calling. Although he enjoyed music, he gave it up to do something he did better—philosophy and writing. Pasternak pursued this with total commitment and kept working on, constantly evolving and refining his craft. From early childhood, he was influenced by such giants as Leo Tolstoy, Austrian poet Rainer Maria Rilke, and Russian composer Alexander Scrirbin.

When the Bolshevik Revolution took place in 1917, he could have fled to Europe but decided to stay in Russia. In 1932, short on money and with no place to live, Pasternak decided to take advantage of one of the perks that the communist regime granted writers—a paid trip in the Ural Mountains. The communist regime felt that Pasternak, as a poet, would "immerse himself in the life of the masses" and "find inspiration."

Pasternak was assigned to a beautiful government dacha, and he ate in a luxurious cafeteria with the political administrators. Outside the compound, people in rags were begging for food. Pasternak couldn't bear the contrast. He saved bread from his meals and gave it to the paupers. He cut his stay short and wrote a frank report and was never sent on a "creative trip" again.

Pasternak could not lie or be dishonest. He showed compassion for others. In the years of Russia's "Great Purge" his life was in danger as he did all he could to help his colleagues who were arrested. He comforted and supported relatives of his executed friends.

"You must always stand your ground," Pasternak wrote one of the widows of an executed comrade, "never let difficulties, however great, get on top of you. Like freedom, because without freedom, it's impossible to open your heart. Live by the principles you've learned in your childhood and listen to and obey your conscience."

In June 1937, Pasternak was asked to sign a joint letter from Soviet writers endorsing the death sentence for eight prominent military figures charged with espionage. He refused, even though his pregnant wife begged him to sign. He knew refusal would mean certain arrest. He abhorred all the killing and couldn't stand it any longer. A colleague forged Pasternak's signature at the last minute.

The communists harshly criticized him for not embracing its ideology and refused to publish his books for long periods. To make a living, he translated the works of Shakespeare and Goethe. He determined not to let the pressure break his spirit. In 1945, he began working on *Doctor Zhivago*. "I cannot postpone the free expression of my real thoughts," he wrote to a cousin. The novel was completed in 1956. Russian publishers rejected it. Finally a copy was smuggled to Italy, and it was published in 1957.

On October 23, 1958, it was announced that Pasternak had won the Swedish Nobel Prize for his writings and especially for *Doctor Zhivago*. The Soviet regime attacked, in the media, *Doctor Zhivago* and called it a "low-grade reactionary hackwork" and called Pasternak a "traitor," a "weed" and a "pig." Pasternak was expelled from the Soviet Writers' Union.

To send a message to the Soviet authorities, he renounced the prize, which was a slap in the face of the authorities. They expected him to grovel and admit his book was a mistake. The tons of verbal mud thrown at him took their toll. Pasternak died in 1960. The film *Doctor Zhivago* went on to win an Academy Award.

CHAPTER 74

Entrepreneur/Wells Fargo

Henry Wells

As a young man, Henry Wells (1805-78) stuttered badly. He tried to overcome the problem but didn't succeed. Large in stature, he often intimidated people with his physical presence. But Wells saw that wouldn't get him very far, so he decided to learn a trade that didn't require much talking. At age 16, he apprenticed as a shoemaker for 3 years.

One day, Wells discovered a speech therapist in Rochester, New York, who helped him to control his stuttering to a degree. But what grabbed his attention was that other students responded better than he did. Seeing an opportunity, Wells decided to open speech therapy schools of his own. He spent the next 15 years expanding to eight cities. He joked later, "I cured everybody but myself."

While traveling to different schools, he noticed people paid large amounts of money to have packages delivered. He started working for a delivery agent overseeing the delivery of packages from Albany to Buffalo, along the Erie Canal in New York and then overland through Pennsylvania, to the Ohio River.

During this time, he built up a lot of good relationships that helped him in later years. In 1841, Wells saw that many people were moving west. He tried to convince an express company owner to set up service westward rather than to Europe. Dismissing Wells proposal, the owner said, "You had better do it on your own account." Wells decided to take that advice, and in 1841, with partners, formed the first several companies doing western express delivery. William Fargo, George Pomeroy and Crawford Livingston became Wells' main partners.

Wells gave 150 percent every day. To deliver packages and freight, he'd use railroads, stagecoaches and anything else that moved. He tried to coordinate deliveries. Wells was not one to set a long list of rules. He told one messenger "Young man, you are bound for Cleveland, and you are expected to get there."

He decided to challenge the post office by charging 6 cents for delivering a letter up to 30 miles or 25 cents up to 400 miles. The government fought him, arresting his messengers. He knew customers responded to a bargain, so he counter-attacked by threatening to deliver letters for 5 cents. Gradually, it forced the government to reduce its rates.

Wells decided to start the first telegraph line in 1845, from New York City to Boston, Buffalo and other cities. By 1850, he could see that the express market was getting crowded. To maintain his share, he united with rivals to form American Express Company. In 1852, Wells and Williams Fargo joined to form Wells, Fargo & Company.

Wells' instincts were dead-on. The company's San Francisco branch was soon booming as it took in gold dust from miners in exchange for money it transferred to the miners' homes back east. The Wells Fargo banking empire had begun. Always looking for opportunities, Wells established a college for women in 1868, in Aurora, New York. For a man of high ideals, it was the dream of his life.

CHAPTER 75

Composer/Musician

Wolfgang Amadeus Mozart

Wolfgang Amadeus Mozart, born in Salzburg, Austria, in 1756, was the youngest of two surviving (of seven) children and the only son of Leopold and Anna Maria Mozart. His elder sister also showed keen musical skills at a young age. Mozart was just 3 years old when he started tinkering with the harpsichord. At age 5, he wrote his first composition and at 9 composed an entire symphony. Many were convinced that he was a fake. They would watch his hands closely. Sometimes he was asked to play unfamiliar songs at a moment's notice.

Mozart didn't pay attention to his critics. He knew what he wanted to do and continued proactively playing and composing. Mozart's father, who was a violinist and assistant conductor, capitalized on his children's talent, taking a three-week tour to Munich in 1772. In June 1773, they took a three-year tour of Europe's capitals.

Mozart had improved to such a degree that he became a giant in musical history. In his 35 years, Mozart produced 27 piano concertos and more than 50 symphonies. His crowning achievements in opera are *The Marriage of Figaro, Don Giovanni, Cosi an Tutee,* and *The Magic Flute.* Mozart had a strong sense of honor. Something he learned from his father who told him, "You know that honor is more important to me than life." He had confidence in his ability and had a sense of mission. He believed that his gifts were God-given and it would be sacrilegious to make light of them.

Mozart became exposed to the best musicians of the day. He spent hours listening to the works of other composers. He mastered musical form and discovered how to draw rich, operatic characters through music. His travels gave him the opportunity to meet Johann Christian Bach, son of Johann Sebastian Bach, Haydn and many others. What he learned benefited him in later works.

To gain financial support, he would dedicate his compositions to prominent people. One British noble gave him 50 guineas after Mozart dedicated six sonatas to him. In 1781, he wrote his father and said, "Apart from my health, I know of nothing more necessary than money." Writing and performing his concertos was his source of income. Mozart had no trouble staying humble. The leisure class didn't consider musicians of the era much better than working-class people.

Though he had his financial ups and downs during his life, he was never a pauper.

As he grew older, he wrote his final and perhaps greatest symphony, the celebrated *Jupiter* in just 16 days. Mozart accomplished all his works in just short of 35 years, dying in Vienna, Austria, in 1791.

CHAPTER 76

Songwriter/Music

Irving Berlin

On the morning of September 23, 1893, the SS *Rhynland* docked at the port of New York. On board were Moses Beline, his wife Lena, and their six children. Hustled to Ellis Island, they were checked for disease. The youngest, 5-year-old Israel Beline, would later change his name to Irving Berlin (1888-1989).

Possessing no lucrative trades, the Belines were poor to the point of desperation but were a close family. The lower East Side was crowded and had terrible living conditions. Inadequate sanitation promoted a variety of diseases like diphtheria, croup, measles, and tuberculosis. These conditions would play a crucial role in Irving Berlin's life and eventually his musical career.

Berlin, born in Mohileu, Russia, would remember the persecution of Jews and the night his home was burned to the ground. His father Moses knew America offered freedom and hope. In Russia, he was a cantor in the synagogue. However, in the U.S. the most he would become was a poultry inspector.

After eight years in New York, the family was in worse condition than at the time of their arrival. In search of freedom, they had gone half around the world and lost a father and daughter in the process. At almost fourteen, Berlin left home. During the next two years he would live in run-down lodging houses.

Berlin's one proven talent was one he inherited from his father, an ability to sing. He would go to the Bowery to sing for 50 cents a night and food and lodging. Eventually, he landed a roll in the chorus of a musicale called *The Show Girl*. His next job was to serve as a "boomer" who was disguised as a paying customer who applauded the chorus and encouraged the audience to sing along. At seventeen, Berlin secured a job at Belham cafe singing ballads and doubling as a singing writer. He never drank or caroused, so he was never one of the boys. Berlin was asked to write songs. He said, "Once you start singing, you start thinking of writing songs, it's as simple as that."

For all his singing experience, he was unable to read or write music. Over the next 60 years, he would dictate to his musical secretary and others. For his first song, he used the pianist to compose "Marie from Sunny Italy." That was published in 1907 and earned him 37 cents as his share. Of greater importance was his name on the title page—I. Berlin.

Irving Berlin's life span was 101 years, which during this time he would write lyrics and music for 1,500 songs. At least 25 would become number one on the music charts. Among them were "Oh How I Hate to Get up in the Morning," which was inspired by his service in the army in 1918, "Alexander's Ragtime Band," "God Bless America," "Annie Get Your Gun," and, of course, "White Christmas"—the most popular song of all time. Irving Berlin's life was a "rags to riches" saga.

CHAPTER 77

Statesman/Philosopher

Benjamin Franklin

B enjamin Franklin was a man of many talents. Born on January 17, 1706, in Boston, Massachusetts, he would attend Boston Grammar School for only two years. He was bound as an apprentice printer to his half brother, James. In 1718, he would publish several newspaper pieces. In September 1723, he ran away to Philadelphia to work in a print shop. A year later, at age 18, he sailed to England where he spent two years. Returning to Philadelphia, in 1726, he went into business, publishing the *Pennsylvania Gazette.*

He married Deborah Read in 1730. They would have three children, and she would prove a great source of strength in business and in his future long service in England and France for government. Franklin's *Poor Richard's Almanac* became the most popular publication in colonial history. It sold ten thousand copies annually for twenty-five years.

A mixture of astrology, recipes, jokes, poems, odd facts and instruction, the almanac would add maxims which included: "Early to bed and early to rise makes a man healthy, wealthy and wise," "A penny saved is a penny earned," and "Keep your eyes wide open before marriage, half shut afterwards."

During the next years, he would be appointed clerk to the

Pennsylvania Assembly and postmaster of Philadelphia, invent the Franklin stove, found the American Philosophical Society, organize a militia against the French, be elected a member of the Pennsylvania Assembly, and pursue scientific interests.

In June 1752, he conducted his famous kite experiment to prove that lightning and electricity were identical. He coined the words "positive" and "negative," "brush," "charge," "conductor," and "armature." Franklin also made the first electrical battery and lightning rod. Honorary graduate degrees were conferred on him from the College of William and Mary, Yale, Harvard, St. Andrews in Scotland, and Oxford in England.

Dr. Franklin taught himself French, Italian, Spanish, Latin, and German. He also learned to play the harp, violin, and guitar. He also invented his own musical instrument called the "harmonica." His personal creed included thirteen virtues: temperance, silence, order, resolution, frugality, industry, sincerity, justice, moderation, cleanliness, tranquility, chastity, and humility. Each week he would focus upon one until mastered.

In June 1757, he sailed for England as an agent of the Pennsylvania Assembly. Over several years, he worked to settle disputes and worked to help repeal the Stamp Act, but in 1774, he sailed home failing to negotiate a peaceful settlement between Great Britain and the Colonies. In May 1775, he was chosen as a delegate to the Second Continental Congress.

On July 2, 1776, the final version of the Declaration of Independence was ready to sign. John Hancock said, "We must be unanimous—there must be no pulling different ways, we must hang together." Franklin then replied, "Yes we must indeed hang together, or must assuredly we shall hang separately." Later Franklin negotiated treaties with France and Great Britain. He died peacefully at home in Philadelphia at age 84. As a young man he wrote his own epitaph.

"The body of Ben Franklin, printer (like the cover of an old book, its contents torn out and stripped of its gilding), lies here, food for worms. But the work shall not be lost: for it will (as he believed) appear once more in a new and more elegant edition revised and corrected by the author."

CHAPTER 78

Inventor/Browning Arms

John M. Browning

John M. Browning was the greatest firearms inventor the world has ever known. Yet little is known about him today. He was the holder of 128 patents covering more than eighty separate and distinct firearms.

Born January 23, 1855, in the small frontier settlement of Ogden, in Utah Territory, John was one of 22 children fathered by Mormon polygamist, Jonathan Browning, a pioneer gunmaker, acquaintance of Abraham Lincoln and manufacturer of many of the guns and implements used in Brigham Young's trek west. Jonathan, who was born October 22, 1805, in Sumner County, Tennessee, was a convert to the Church of Jesus Christ of Latter-Day Saints. Browning moved to Quincy, Illinois, then later on to Nauvoo, Illinois, after his conversion, and eventually out west. At age 7, John showed interest in following his father in gunsmithing. At ten, he took the smashed barrel of an old flintlock stick of wood, a piece of wire, and a scrap of tin and fashioned them into a makeshift gun. Taking some of his father's powder and shot, he went out and shot some prairie chickens.

John made his first gun, a single-shot rifle in 1878, when he was 23 years old. The marking read: J.M. Browning-Ogden, Utah, April 10, 1879. He married Rachel Teresa Child on June 21, 1879.

When his father, Jonathan, died in his eighty-fourth year, John and his brothers built a new gunshop and installed the machinery. The first guns were produced and then sold in one week for $25 each. Sometime in early 1883, a Winchester Repeating Arms employee came across one of the Brownings' guns. TG Bennett, vice president of Winchester, traveled from New Haven, Connecticut, to Ogden. A deal was struck for $8,000, plus he would place Browning on the Winchester jobbing list. An agreement was reached for $1,000 down and the balance in 30 days. The agreement set an example that would be followed in all subsequent negotiations. No contract was ever drawn up by a lawyer. Within a few years, Winchester would become the largest producer of sporting arms in the U.S. with almost all firearms from Browning inventions.

Browning would go on to develop the Browning automatic rifle (B.A.R) for the military. It would be used in World Wars I and II, plus the Korean War. From machine guns, shotguns, cannons, .45 caliber pistols, his guns were manufactured by Browning, Remington, Savage, Marlin, Stevens, and Westinghouse. Later he would go to Liege, Belgium, to produce pistols and shotguns for Fabrique Nationale.

In the forty-seven years between the first patent and his death, he set the basic trends in repeating rifles, shotguns, machine guns, automatic rifles, automatic pistols, and military small arms, both gas and recoil operated. Over 30 million Browning-designed guns were produced up to 1964.

Awards included the John Scott legacy medal by the city of Philadelphia, a decoration by King Albert of Belgium for the Cross of Knighthood of the Order of Leopold. Henceforth, he would be called Sir John M. Browning.

John Moses Browning died in Liege, Belgium, in November 26, 1926, the greatest firearms inventor the world has ever known. A final tribute to the man who contributed so much to national security was given by the secretary of War with a military escort and a draped American flag.

CHAPTER 79

Explorer/Loyalty

Sir Ernest Shackleton

Ernest Shackleton (1874-1922) was a bright young man but not much of a student. School bored him so he found interest in *The Boys Own Paper,* a paper directed to young boys. It had stories of moral uplift, true adventure, fiction, patriotism and blood and thunder serials. These tales whetted his taste for adventure.

Just after reaching age 16, Shackleton left school and joined the Merchant Marines. For the next 10 years, he sailed all over the world and moved up in the ranks. However, the life of a sailor did not satisfy him. In 1901, the Royal Society and the Royal Geographical Society were planning an expedition to Antarctica. Navy officer Robert Scott would be in command. Shackelton applied for, and became, second in command.

He spent the next two years in Antarctica. Scott knew nothing about polar exploration and, as a result, the expedition failed to reach the South Pole. Shackleton decided he'd lead a trip himself after he got home. He started raising funds and vowed not to repeat Scott's mistakes.

First, he set out to pick the right men. He wanted five things attributed to his men, in order of importance: optimism, patience, physical endurance, idealism, and courage. Part of the reason Scott's expedition went poorly was that the men were poorly nourished and weak from scurvy. He hired a skilled cook to keep the party well fed. As a result, none of his men suffered from scurvy.

Shackleton's style was informal. He delegated well and took and interest in each man. He made them feel important. He never asked his men to do anything he wouldn't do. Shackleton left for Antarctica in 1907. For two years they mapped parts never seen before.

Returning to England, he started to plan immediately for another expedition, leaving in 1914. In the Antarctica waters, ice flows trapped and crushed Shackleton's ship. For five months they lived on the ice, sleeping in shifts, as anytime the ice could break beneath them, sending men into the frigid sea. The men endured temperatures so low, they could hear the water freeze. The bitter cold froze their garments solid. They slept in tents so thin that they could see the moon through them. Stuck 1,200 miles from the nearest outpost, their chances of rescue were slim.

Finally, the ice gave way and they set out in small lifeboats. For two weeks, they sailed across stormy seas to Elephant Island, which was barely big enough to hold the men. So Shackleton took another boat and made for the nearest inhabited island. For 16 days, he and a small party sailed across stormy-swept seas before making land. Landing on the wrong side of the island, he hiked over the snow-capped mountains to the whaling station.

Shackleton insisted on going back to Elephant Island to rescue and bring back all of his men alive. Shackleton combined nerve, intelligence, and overwhelming commitment to his men. He had marched closer to the South Pole than any man before him, for this he was knighted.

CHAPTER 80

Scientist/Inventor

Charles Steinmetz

Karl August Rudolph Steinmetz (his real name) was born on April 9, 1865, in Breslau, Germany. His mother died from cholera in 1866. Grandmother Steinmetz took the place of his mother. She pampered and spoiled her grandson who, like his father, was deformed physically. Charles was a hunchbacked, crippled dwarf.

Karl hated kindergarten, and it was decided he would not have to attend. A year later, at age 5, his father demanded that he go back to school. Being a year older, he did like school. At age 8, he was sent to St. John's Gymnasium, which was a classical high school that prepared students for the university. One day the headmaster told his father, "I don't like to tell you this, Mr. Steinmetz, but it seems to me and all Karl's teachers that he is not very bright. He can't do the multiplication tables, you'll have to resign yourself to the fact he is not only physically handicapped, but mentally retarded as well." A transformation took place the next year, and at age 10, he was considered the brightest pupil at St. John's. At age 17, he took top honors at graduation examinations. Karl enrolled at the University of Breslau, and there excelled in mathematics. At the university, he developed his own phonetics shorthand. It was here that students gave him his middle name Proteus after a sea god.

The secret police were shadowing him because of his political activities so he left Germany for Zurich, Switzerland, where he earned a degree at Zurich Polytechnic School. While attending class, he met Oscar Asmussen. One night Oscar described the opportunities in the United States. The two of them bought steerage tickets and sailed into New York, June 1, 1889.

Steinmetz applied for a position at the Edison plant and was told, "There's nothing here for you." Going to Yonkers, he secured a job in a hat factory, run by Rudolph Eickenmeyer, as a draftsman. Soon he was working in the laboratory. Eickenmeyer recognized his superior knowledge and made him his assistant in charge of the whole plant.

During this time, he produced and improved an electric motor for Otis Elevator Company, which made it possible for the erection of skyscrapers. Steinmetz solved the problem of "Hyseresis" in 1891, which involved the reversal of electric motors hesitation and motors overheating. With it, direct current was doomed, and alternating current would become the standard. During this time he changed his name to Charles Proteus Steinmetz to sound more American.

Edison Light Company and Thomson-Houston merged to become General Electric. Soon after, Eickenmeyer had an offer from this new company. At first, Steinmetz refused to leave for G.E., but later relented. There he designed a more practical and efficient transformer that would work under all conditions.

Steinmetz was made chief of the calculating department. There was no math problem that he could not solve. Five years had passed and he could now become a U.S. citizen, of which he was more proud of than his inventions.

Steinmetz improved the arc light and put them on the streets of Schenectady, New York. He became a professor of Union College in 1903 and was awarded a degree of Doctor of Philosophy.

After his improvement of the mercury arc lamp, he devoted his time to the long-distance transmission of electricity by using alternating current. He was involved in the improvement of local schools. He advocated the use of hydroelectric power by harnessing the nation's rivers. He solved the problems of lightning knocking out transmission lines with an improved lightning arrestor.

On October 26, 1923, Charles Proteus Steinmetz died. The wizard of Schenectady, the hunchbacked, crippled dwarf, was a genius of electrical engineering and mathematics and a superman of the electrical age.

CHAPTER 81

Inventor/Scientist

Thomas Alva Edison

Thomas Alva Edison (1847-1931) as a child tried to learn everything he could about any subject. He was always asking questions in order to satisfy his curiosity. He set fires to see how flames traveled and consumed different materials. Once, he accidentally burned down the family barn.

Edison's teachers concluded that his questioning showed a lack of intelligence. But his mother had faith in him, and at age 8 started teaching him at home. To make money for his experiments and family, he went to work at age 12, selling candy and newspapers. Young Edison soon became the family's chief source of income.

At age 16, Edison was working as a railroad telegrapher. In between sending signals every half hour for just one train on his shift, he invented an automatic signaler so he could spend his time reading and fiddling with his early inventions.

In 1869, he decided to go to New York with $1 to his name. He hunted jobs by day and slept in the basement of the Gold Indicator Co. by night. When the company's new gold price indicator failed, Edison fixed it. Pleased company officials gave him a job. Soon he had improved the machine so that all the tickers could be adjusted from the central office. He was paid $40,000 for the invention.

Putting his money to work, Edison started American Telegraph Works in Newark, New Jersey. To ensure that the company was strong, he hired the most skilled engineers he could find. He stacked the building with every top science book published. Later, in 1876, he built the first industrial laboratory in Menlo Park, New Jersey. Edison often worked deep into the night and fell asleep at his workbench. Sometimes his wife wouldn't see him for days. "A minor invention every 10 days," he demanded from his staff.

To drum up investment money for his lightbulb project, in 1878, he invited a local newspaper to report in the progress. The platinum filament he used at the time only lasted a few minutes, so he wisely turned it off before it burned out. Impressed, the reporter wrote an exciting article, and soon investors were calling Edison with the capital he needed to find a longer-burning filament. Team members tried more than 150 materials and nothing worked. Other scientists and inventors scoffed at Edison's efforts. After everyone else was ready to give up, Edison, in 1879, tried a carbonized cardboard filament. It burned nearly 200 hours and the lightbulb was born.

Edison's hearing had been fading ever since 8 years old. He'd been asked to improve Alexander Graham Bell's invention of the telephone. How could he do it without being able to hear? Realizing that sound was vibrations, he hit upon a magnet attached to the phone. This allowed the sounds to go through his teeth and vibrate the tiny bones in his inner ear. His invention, a carbon transmitter, made it possible to market Bell's telephone on a massive scale.

Edison was responsible, jointly and individually, for 1,093 patents. Besides the lightbulb, he invented the phonograph, first motion picture camera, first electrical generated system, carbon telephone transmitter, and cement mixer. He said, "The brain can be developed, if only one will take the pains to train the mind to think." "Society is never prepared to receive any new invention," he said. "Every new thing is resisted and it takes years for the inventor to get people to listen to him and years more before it can be introduced."

CHAPTER 82

Humorist/Cowboy

Will Rogers

Will Rogers was born on November 4, 1879, in Oogogah, Oklahoma. Part Cherokee Indian, he was proud of his heritage. In later years, he admitted that his ancestors didn't come over on the *Mayflower*, but he said, "They met the boat." The Cherokees were farmers, merchants, and cattlemen. They lived in houses and learned to read and write because of their contacts with settlers.

As a young man, Will learned to ride and throw the lariat. He practiced throwing his rope, and soon was good enough to rope cattle for branding. Not one to love schooling, he dropped out of Kemper Military Academy at 17. He was keen of memory and could recite the Gettysburg Address and Patrick Henry's speech "Give me liberty or give me death."

Working as a ranch hand, he took jobs driving cattle. Eventually he would end up delivering mules to South Africa. While there, he got a job in Texas Jack's Wild West Circus using his skill with lariat. He could do the "crinoline," which involved letting out all of the rope in a big loop. He took the title of "The Cherokee Kid."

Will Rogers didn't smoke, drink, or gamble. After traveling to South Africa and Argentina, he took up doing rope shows. Rogers would talk humorously in between rope throws. He trained his horse Teddy to run across the stage while he lassoed him. Later he bought a blue blanket with a gold band and had the name "Will Rogers" placed on it.

Married November 25, 1908, he promised to settle down and give up stage life. That didn't last very long. Soon he was signed for an act with the Ziegfield Follies. His humor and rope were the tricks of his trade. He liked to make fun of politics in his show. Rogers said, "You have to admit that each party looks worse than the other—the one that is out always looks the best."

In 1918, Rogers made his debut in motion pictures, which were silent movies at the time. Later he wrote a Sunday article for the *New York Times* and the *McNaugh Syndicate*. His folksy down-to-earth philosophy and humor brought enjoyment to readers. One quote was, "I was raised on a little ranch and I never heard of a ranchman going broke—only the ones who borrowed money." Another favorite was, "I don't make jokes, I just watch the government and report the facts and I have never found it necessary to exaggerate." One truth Rogers said was, "You loan a man money and you lose his friendship."

When his sister Maude passed away, uninformed newspapers wrote, "Mrs. C.L. Lane, sister of comedian Will Rogers, died." Will felt it was the other way around. He wrote, "I am the brother of Mrs. C.L. Lane, the friend of humanity" in tribute to her memory. "All the honors that I could ever hope to reach would never equal the honor on a little western prairie hilltop, among her people. If they love me like that at my finish, my life will not have been in vain."

Rogers never earned a college degree and refused all honorary degrees. He made it a policy never to gossip. When an absent person was raked over the coals by a group, Will would find something to say in their favor. He wouldn't pick on anyone who was down.

Will Rogers loved to fly, so when Wiley Post asked him to fly to Alaska with him, he accepted. Post had twice flown around the world. On August 15, 1935, in a dense fog, just 15 miles from point Barrow, their plane crashed. Both men were killed.

CHAPTER 83

Scientist/Chemist

George Washington Carver

George Washington Carver (1864-1943) was born a slave and raised on a farm near Diamond Grove, Missouri. Since there were no schools in his town, he used an old Webster blue-black speller and studied the alphabet until he knew it by heart. He taught himself to read and write.

Carver had a great interest in nature, collecting plants and rocks. He built his own green house, spending hours each day studying the needs of plants. He nursed sickly ones back to health with proper nutrients and water. Carver was nicknamed "The Plant Doctor."

Curious about nature, Carver asked himself questions like "What is rain? What makes it? What are hail and snow? Why are geraniums red?" and "Why is black soil better than yellow soil?" At age 11, he attended an all-black school studying and reading to stimulate his mind. The commitment paid off by winning entrance to Simpson College in Indianola, Iowa. Transferring to Iowa Agricultural College in Ames, Iowa, he earned a masters degree and became a professor. Soon he was an agricultural scientist.

In 1896, Tuskegee Institute founder Booker T. Washington asked him to head the school's agricultural department.

At the time an insect, the boll weevil, was devastating cotton crops. Cotton also depleted the soil of important nutrients. After studying the problem, Carver introduced crop rotation in 1915, planting peanuts one year and cotton the next. Greater harvests resulted. The abundance of large quantities of peanuts created a need for new uses of peanuts.

Doing experiments, he heated the peanuts and put them under a press to produce a cup of oil. Taking the dry cake left from the pressed oil, he added water, set up an artificial digestion process and found the cake loaded with protein. Further experiments with peanuts emitted a milk-like fluid. He separated peanuts into such by-products as fats, oils, gums, resins, pectins, sugars, starches and amino acids. The results complete, Carver found he could create margarine, cooking oil, rubbing oil, milk, and cosmetics.

Carver would produce more than 300 products from peanuts at Tuskegee. They included beverages, sauces, salve, bleach, paper, plastics, shaving cream, synthetic rubber, printer's ink, and face powder. Other tests on sweet potatoes, soybeans, and pecans found over 20 uses for these crops.

Awards were given. Carver was named a fellow of the Royal Society of Arts in London in 1916. In 1923, he received the Spingarn Medal from the National Association for the Advancement of Colored People and the Theodore Roosevelt Medal of Science in 1939.

He willed his entire life savings to Tuskegee in 1943. Carver wasn't interested in profiting from his products but in benefiting others. The epitaph on his grave reads, "He could have added fortune to fame, but caring for neither, he found happiness and honor in being helpful to the world."

CHAPTER 84

Motivator/Author

Napolean Hill

Napolean Hill (1883-1970) was born in a one-room log cabin. As a youngster, he was often hungry. There was a time when he ate bark scraped off birch trees.

Hill began his writing career as a 13-year-old "mountain reporter" for a small-town newspaper. He would go on to become one of the best motivational authors of all time, achieving great success as an attorney and journalist.

As a young man, Hill began to study great achievers such as Thomas Edison and Alexander Graham Bell. It was during an interview with Andrew Carnegie, the steel millionaire, that Carnegie gave him a challenge. The challenge was, "Would one be willing to spend the next twenty years or more preparing himself to take Carnegie's money-making secret to the world?" It was Mr. Carnegie's idea that the magic formula be placed within the reach of people. He believed the formula should be taught in all public schools and colleges, that it could revolutionize the entire educational system, and that the time spent in school could be reduced to less than half.

Hill took the challenge and started interviewing successful people. Many admitted that they had accumulated their vast fortunes through the aid of the Carnegie secret. Among these men were Henry Ford, William Wrigley, John D. Rockefeller, F.W. Woolworth, King Gillette, George Eastman, and dozens of others. The results of his interviews were incorporated in *Think and Grow Rich,* one of the most influential books of all time. The book points the way to personal achievement and financial independence. It covered subjects such as desire, faith, visualization, auto suggestion, imagination, organization, procrastination, persistence, fear, and the sixth sense.

Since its publication in 1937, over 20 million copies have been sold. Hill said, "If you have ever had difficulties to surmount which took the very soul out of you, if you ever tried and failed, if you were ever handicapped by illness or physical affliction, then the magic formula can help you. The philosophy cannot be had without a price, as there is not such thing as something for nothing."

Hill went on to write other books. But his *Think and Grow Rich* stands out today as the bible for personal achievement. Thousands have discovered the magic formula.

CHAPTER 85

Adventurer/President

Theodore Roosevelt

Theodore Roosevelt (1858-1919) was born into a prominent New York family. He was constantly suffering from ailments including headaches, fevers, stomach pains, upset intestines, and asthma attacks. They were so intense, they suffocated him. The ailments could last for weeks.

At the time, no medicines existed to open the passages in his lungs and bring relief from the rasping, labored struggle for air. Home remedies didn't work. Finally his father told him to build up his strength working out in the gym. Working on weights, parallel bars and boxing, he gradually built up his body. He also kept busy drawing pictures of mice and birds, plus reading adventure books of the American West, and climbing mountains. Eventually, his asthma attacks subsided.

In the summer of 1872, Teddy Roosevelt was given his first pair of spectacles and a 12-gauge shotgun. It changed the 13-year-old boy's life forever. Teddy's confidence flourished. A few years later, at Harvard, the asthma returned. The college physician told him he had a heart condition and must lead a quiet life, choose a sedentary occupation, and avoid strenuous exertion. Roosevelt told the doctor he could never live that way and vowed to do exactly the opposite.

Instead, Roosevelt headed west with his brother on a hunting trip. Later Roosevelt married his long-time sweetheart, Alice, in October of 1880. He bought a cattle ranch in the Dakota Territory. He was then elected as a New York Assembly man. He was viewed as a rising star in the Republican Party. On February 14, 1884, Alice died during childbirth. Devastated by the loss, he spent more time at his ranch in North Dakota. There he wrote his first book, *Hunting Trips of a Ranchman.*

Once, he rode up to see one of his cowboys about to burn the Roosevelt brand on an unbranded stray found on someone else's range. He terminated the man on the spot. Roosevelt said, "A man who will steal for me will also steal from me." Once, he covered 72 miles on horseback in a single day. His horse, along with his 47-75 Winchester rifle, allowed him to slip back in time and pleased him. Life on the ranch had helped him overcome ill health.

In 1898, he led the Rough Riders charging up San Juan Hill in the Spanish-American War. He became a hero and was elected governor of New York. In 1900, Roosevelt was elected vice president and became president in 1901.

Roosevelt focused on preserving public lands and advocating intelligent, multiple use of federal land. The nation acquired several of its most scenic parks and national monuments under his tenure. He worked to fight loggers who cut everything in sight and helped bring about national forests.

From a sick youngster, he had grown into a vigorous individual. Roosevelt left a legacy of protected wildlife refuges, national forests, grasslands, monuments and wilderness areas. He also worked for railroad regulation and protection of the public against harmful foods.

CHAPTER 86

Persistence/Peacemaker

Mohandas Gandhi

Mohandas Gandhi (1869-1948) was born in Porbander, India. Gandhi's father was a shrewd politician known for his loyalty and impartiality in settling disputes. His mother practiced self-denial, giving willingly to the service of others.

At age 13, he married a pretty and strong-willed girl named Kasturbal. Child marriages were a Hindu custom, with parents arranging them. The marriage lasted 62 years. Mohandas was a vegetarian for religious reasons.

One incident gave him his first lesson in non-violence. Mohandas had stolen some gold from home. In shame, he wrote a confession and handed it to his father. Reading it, Gandhi's father cried and then embraced him. He learned that truthful repentance had the power to inspire forgiveness instead of angry punishment. This principle would shape his adult life.

Not yet 19, Gandhi sailed for England in September 1888, to study law for three years. On his return to India, he soon realized that studying law was not the same as how to practice it. Worst of all, he lacked the ability to speak in public. Without good prospects in his own country, Gandhi took an offer with a concern in the British Colony of South Africa. The firm needed someone with the knowledge of English and law to represent them.

It would prove to be a new beginning. Traveling by train to Pretoria, a white man entered the first-class compartment in which Gandhi was sitting, stared at him and left. He returned with two officials who told him to go to the third-class car. Gandhi insisted he had a first-class ticket. When Gandhi refused to move, he was pushed off the train with his luggage. Should he stay and fight for his rights, or give up and go back to India? He chose to stay and fight against race prejudice. It was a night that changed the course of his life.

His passive resistance became a hallmark of ideology. He soon became a leader of the Indian community. Gandhi realized that for his message to get through he'd have to couch it in words that everyone could understand. Using the potent power of Hindu religious practices, he enlisted mass support.

Gandhi tried to inspire people by addressing them in positive terms. He didn't speak about how bad the British were, instead, he chose to talk about the greatness of the cause of India's independence from the beginning. He aimed all his efforts at leading the Indian community to independence. It was a difficult task as there was strife between Hindu's various castes and Muslims. Gandhi said, "All Indians, Hindus, Muslims, Jews, and Christians alike should be allowed to follow their own religions." For strategy, Gandhi chose the term "satyagraha"—the force of truth and love, which was to refrain from violence, think well of opponents, officials and jailers. In March, 1830, Gandhi set out on a 24-day Salt March to the coast with thousands joining him. The British controlled all salt production. He had broken the law that made it illegal to obtain salt, except through the British. Gandhi's act proved to be a powerful non-violent demonstration that India was impatient and ready for self-rule. India was eventually granted its independence on August 15, 1947, but Gandhi didn't live to enjoy his triumph for very long. On January 30, 1948, a man assassinated him. Gandhi became known by the honorific title "Mahatma" (Great Soul) for helping to force the British out of his country.

CHAPTER 87

Director/Movies

John Ford

John Ford was born John Feeney on February 1, 1894, on a farm near Cape Elizabeth, Maine. As a youth, he loved the sea and told himself that one day he would be an admiral and sail the mighty oceans.

At eight, an attack of diphtheria put him a year behind in school. So at home, he became a voracious reader, which helped him develop a creative mind. His favorite pastime was going to the nickelodeons and movies. Loving the glamour of the movies, he worked as an usher in the theaters.

In 1910, John entered Portland High School where football was his passion. At six feet two and 175 pounds, he could play halfback, fullback, and defensive tackle. He was hoping to enter Annapolis, but he failed the entrance examination.

His fascination with the movies was enhanced when he saw his brother Francis do less acting and more directing. In 1914, John decided to follow his brother to California. Dreaming of becoming a writer, he took the name of John Ford to associate himself with Francis Ford, who had changed his name from Feeney. From now on Jack Feeney would be known as John Ford.

Securing a job at Universal, he earned twelve dollars a week. Later, an advancement to assistant property manager earned him fifteen dollars a week. By 1916, John Ford had become an assistant director in charge of extras and cowboys. Within a year, he was directing his own pictures.

"I believe in the 'American Dream' and think if you work hard enough you will succeed," he declared. In the following years, he directed such classics as *Stagecoach* with John Wayne and Claire Trevor, *The Grapes of Wrath* starring Henry Fonda and Jane Darwell, *How Green Was My Valley, Drums along the Mohawk, She wore a Yellow Ribbon,* and many others for a total of 136 pictures. A genius with the camera, he had the ability to capture the magnificence of western landscape, especially Monument Valley, Utah.

Having made a series of U.S. Navy Films, on September 12, 1934, he was appointed a lieutenant commander in the Naval Reserve. In April 1940, Ford created, without official sanction, a naval reserve unit of professional filmmakers. He knew that the U.S. would become involved in war and wanted to be ready.

By February 1947, he was requested to take pictures of the war in the Pacific. Three days after arriving at the American base at Midway, the Japanese attack began. Filming it, he was hit by shrapnel. The siege lasted until June 6, when the U.S. defeated the Japanese attack. The holding of Midway allowed the U.S. control of the central Pacific. From that, he was promoted to commander. The footage taken became "The Battle of Midway" and boosted morale on the home front.

Ford was there, with his unit, at the invasion of North Africa and the invasion at Normandy, France. Over this time he lost 13 of the crew. Later he would realize his ambition and was appointed a rear admiral.

John Ford won six Academy Awards, four New York film critics awards, and, from the navy, the Legion of Merit and the Purple Heart. John Ford remains the most honored director in Hollywood history. Ford died August 31, 1973, in Palm Springs, California.

CHAPTER 88

Colonizer/Leader

Brigham Young

Brigham Young was born on June 1, 1801, in Whittingham, Vermont. The ninth child of an indigent farmer, he received no formal schooling. He grew to manhood on the heavily wooded lands of central New York State. Being poor, his life consisted of picking up brush, chopping down trees, rolling logs, clearing land to farm and doing household chores. His father taught him strict moral values and he studied the Bible.

Brigham's mother died when he was 14 years old. By age 16, he had become an apprentice, carpenter, joiner, painter, and glazier. At age 23, he married and had two daughters. Brigham and his wife joined the Methodist Church. In 1831, his wife Miriam contracted tuberculosis. Brigham took over the household duties. In September 1832, his wife died.

Young wrestled with religious questions. He sought a church organized according to the pattern Jews had established in the New Testament, with a system of ordinances. In April 1830, Young's brothers and sisters obtained two copies of the Book of Mormon. They believed its contents, but Brigham did not immediately accept it. After two more years he was baptized on April 15, 1832. Brigham was anxious to meet the Prophet Joseph Smith, and traveled to Kirtland, Ohio, to meet him. He became the presiding authority of the Church of Jesus Christ of Latter-Day Saints in 1844, following the death of Joseph Smith.

A few years later, when church members were expelled from Nauvoo, Illinois, and were wintering in Iowa and Nebraska, he received revelation outlining the way to move the membership to the West. Arriving in the Salt Lake Valley, he proclaimed, "This is the right place."

After becoming established in the Great Basin, he sent missionaries abroad to Europe, the South Pacific, Scandinavia, India, South America, Asia, and the West Indies. He founded industries for products unavailable in the West, such as iron, silk, and sugar. He was appointed Governor of the Utah Territory in 1851, started a newspaper, the *Deseret News*, in June 1850, and established the University of Deseret in 1850 (later the University of Utah), and Brigham Young Academy in 1875 (later Brigham Young University).

Brigham Young colonized much of the West. By 1877, over 350 settlements had been organized in what are now the states of California, Nevada, Utah, Idaho, Wyoming, Arizona, and New Mexico. By the time of his death in August 29, 1877, Young had married 27 women who bore him a total of 57 children. (Plural marriage was discontinued in 1890 in order for Utah to gain statehood.)

Young was a modern-day Moses, having led thousands of followers to the arid Salt Lake Valley where there were few trees, timber, or freshwater. Without any political and financial backing, he established, from scratch in the desert, an ordered and industrious society, he made the "desert blossom as a rose."

CHAPTER 89

Determination/Athlete

Mildred "Babe" Didrikson Zaharias

Mildred Didrikson made a promise as a child. She determined to become the best woman athlete in the world. Born in June 26, 1914, in Port Arthur, Texas, Mildred achieved her first athletic achievement when she was just 16 years old. She was named an all-American high school basketball player.

As a lanky "tomboy," Didrikson played all kinds of sports with her brothers. She played baseball with the neighborhood boys and soon found out that she could run faster, jump higher and throw a baseball farther than any of them. The boys said Mildred can throw as well as Babe Ruth, a nickname that stayed with her throughout the years.

She believed that she inherited her physical coordination from her mother, who had been one of the best women skiers and skaters in Norway before emigrating to America. Learning to play the harmonica, Babe would join the family orchestra on the front porch at night—the boys on the drums, the girls on the piano and violin. The neighbors would sit on the porch and listen.

Determined to earn a place in the U.S. track team, Babe entered the track meet at Northwestern University in Evanston, Illinois. She represented the Golden Cyclones, and she was the only representative. Most of the teams had 15 to 20 members. How could she win against such odds? At 105 pounds and five feet six, she was not a brawny athlete. Still, she had registered to compete in 8 of the 10 events.

Entering the disc event, she took fourth place. In the shot put, Babe took first place. In the baseball throw, another first. In the Javelin toss, the broad jump and the eighty meter hurdles, she was the winner. She tied for first with Jean Shiley in the high jump. At the end of the meet, Babe had 30 points and the Chicago Athletic Club, with twenty-two participants, took second. Babe had won the whole track meet by herself and qualified for the 1932 Olympics.

In California, the tenth Olympiad came at last (1938). In the javelin throw, Babe set a new record of 143 feet 5 inches to win her first gold medal. Winning the preliminary event in the eighty-meter hurdles, she went on to win the final race and another gold medal. In the high jump, Babe won a silver medal.

Grantland Rice, sports columnist, invited her to play golf. So they went to a practice course where she hit the ball so hard it went 250 yards. Intrigued by the sport, Babe entered the Fort Worth Women's Invitational Tournament where she shot a seventy-seven, but she was eliminated in the second round. Every sport Dallas had to offer, Babe had tried. She excelled at softball, billiards, aquaplane, and diving, but golf offered a big challenge. Persistence paid off, and in 1948 she captured the U.S. Women's Open title. She married George Zaharias in December 23, 1938.

By the time she was twenty, Babe had won 635 championships in 636 competitions and was called the greatest all-around woman athlete. After many championships, she was able to conquer all but cancer, dying September 27, 1956. The Associated Press named her "The Greatest Women's Athlete of the First Half of the Century."

CHAPTER 90

Inventor/Lear Jet

William Lear

William Lear was born in 1902 in Hannibal, Missouri, a child of immigrant parents and a broken home. As a youth, he avidly read Horatio Alger's "rags to riches" books, as well as anything he could find about radio, electricity and airplanes. Lear spent lots of time in libraries reading about technical innovations.

Despite his thirst for knowledge, he left school after the eighth grade to go to work as a mechanic at age 12. He wrote out a plan for his life to become an inventor. Lear's ability to follow through on his ideas was his strong point, where other inventors relied on someone else to market their ideas. Lear would carry out the idea all the way to the market. Lear figured out what he wanted, then devised a way to get it.

To further his knowledge he joined the navy and worked as a radio operator around the end of World War I. Wanting to learn to fly, he paid for lessons by building radios. In 1922, he started the Quincy Radio Laboratories in Quincy, Illinois. Later, Lear moved to Tulsa, Oklahoma, to form Lear Radio Laboratory. By age 24, most of his efforts were futile and had not met with success.

Not one to give up easily, Lear had a great sense of humor, which carried him through some of the disappointments in business. Keeping an eye on the latest trends, he saw that the automobile would one day be popular, and people would want radios in them. Lear started working on a radio small enough to fit in a car. By the mid-1920s, he completed his goal and dubbed it the "Motorola," which was a big success. Later, he sold his stake to the manufacturer, Robert Galvin, whose firm was later named Motorola.

After selling Motorola, Lear launched Lear Development Co. to make components for car radios. He developed an amplifier design which he sold to Radio Corporation of America. In 1934, he founded Lear Avia Corporation to develop radio gear and direction finders for airplanes. By 1939, more than half of all private planes were outfitted by Lear's company.

Lear believed a solution existed to every problem; it was just a matter of perspective. He believed in keeping things simple. Constantly looking for a better way, he devised a small autopilot that weighed only 24 pounds. He also invented the eight-track stereo cartridges. By the late 1950s, Lear decided to build a baby jet that would be small, fast and perfect for corporate needs, though he had never built a plane. The Lear Corporation Board disagreed with his idea, so he sold out and started a new company, Lear Jet Corporation, in 1962. By 1963, his prototype business jet made its first flight. By 1968, Lear Jet had sold $90 million worth of planes.

Lear's philosophy of life was, "Don't tell me it can't be done", and he would set out to prove others wrong. Lear earned 150 patents during his lifetime. As an inventor, he had the ability to follow through on his ideas. William Lear's work continued until age 75 when he died in 1978 in Reno, Nevada.

CHAPTER 91

Industrialist/Manufacturer

George Westinghouse

George Westinghouse was born in a village called Central Bridge in New York, October 6, 1846. As a young child, George would use temper tantrums to get his way by stamping his feet, screaming or banging his head on the wall. His older brothers liked to tease him to see what actions he would take. He didn't like the routine and confinement of school, but he enjoyed visiting his father's shop.

Outside the school season, he worked for 50 cents a day at age 13. Working on little gadgets of his own, he got in trouble with his father for not working on the projects assigned. In 1861, the Civil War started and Westinghouse signed up for the Calvary at age 16. After some months of scouting, he transferred to the Navy serving on the ship *Muscoota, Stars and Stripes,* and other smaller ships.

In 1865, the war ended, and he entered Union College. Spending most of his time thinking about inventions instead of studies, he began tinkering on a steam engine of his own design. He eventually received a patent on his rotary steam engine. Soon he left college to work for his father. That same year he developed a device for improving railroad "frogs" to keep cars on the correct rails at intersections and track switches. The old ones kept wearing out. Westinghouse invented reversible frogs so they could be turned over when one side wore out, and he made them of cast steel. Fortunately, his railroad frogs sold by the thousands.

While on a train trip from Schenectady to Troy, his train slowed to a stop. Up ahead two freight trains had collided, the hand brakes could not stop the trains in time. After reading about the use of compressed air for tunnel drilling, he developed a system that allowed the air to go through pipes and hoses to all the cars. Each car had its own brakes. When the air was applied, it kept the brakes open, and when the air pressure dropped, the brakes clamped down to stop the train. The Westinghouse system became the standard of the industry.

By 1892, Westinghouse submitted the lowest bid to light up the Chicago World's Columbian Exhibition. Setting up 12 electric generators, each the size of a locomotive, and using Tesla's electric motors with alternating current, he was able to light up 8,000 arc lights and 130,000 lightbulbs. Due to the success of this installation, Westinghouse was awarded the contract for harnessing the power of Niagara Falls. By 1896, three 5,000 horsepower alternating current generators were producing power from the falls. Soon power lit up the city of Buffalo, 20 miles away. Over time it serviced a large section of New York. From that project, alternating current stations spread across the country.

Eventually Westinghouse founded 60 companies based on his inventions which altogether totaled 361 patents. He was respected for his interest in fellow inventors and generous benefits he gave to thousands of employees. Of all his accomplishments, Westinghouse simply said, "If someday they say of me that in my work I have contributed something to the welfare and happiness of my fellow men, I shall be satisfied."

He died March 12, 1914, at age 67. He and wife Marguerite were survived by one son named George, like his father and grandfather before him.

CHAPTER 92

Inventor

Nikola Tesla

Nikola Tesla was born in 1856, in the province of Lika in Croatia. His original family's name was Draganic. The name Tesla was a trade name like Smith and Carpenter.

In childhood, he and other boys built a smooth waterwheel, a device that contained inherent concepts that would later form the basis of Tesla's innovative bladeless steam turbines, and a cornstalk popgun, which contained principles he later adapted when he fashioned particle-beam weapons. Always experimenting, a jump off a barn with a parasol laid him up for six weeks.

Tesla inherited his father's sense of humor. He was known to talk to himself and was able to develop his memory and recite works in several languages. In 1880, Tesla enrolled at the University of Prague, where he studied mathematics, philosophy, and mechanical theory. After his schooling, he moved to Budapest, Hungary, and worked in the central telegraph offices as a draftsman and designer. He then moved onto Paris where he worked for Continental Edison in 1884. Tesla sailed for America when he was 28 years old and went to work for Edison. By this time, he had studied a dozen languages, delved into literature and art, and studied in many libraries. His academic training and mathematical skills had given him a great advantage over Edison's trial-and-error system of invention. However, he was unsuccessful in persuading Edison on the alternating current (AC) motor.

Failing to convince Edison of the better motor, Tesla left his employment. In March 1885, Tesla organized his own company and applied for his first patent on an improved design of the ARC lamp. He installed the first and only arc-lighting system in Rawway, New Jersey, and it won rave reviews for Tesla Electric Light and Manufacturing. Unfortunately, his partners did not share the goal of developing the AC motor, and he was forced out. Bankrupt, he was forced to do menial labor digging ditches.

With new partners, he formed Tesla Electric Company, producing three complete systems of AC machinery—for single-phase, two-phase, and three-phase currents. They began producing AC induction motors. In July 1888, George Westinghouse agreed to purchase Tesla's AC motors and a total of 40 of his patents for approximately $255,000.

In 1892, Tesla unveiled the first radio. He expanded his high-intensity button lamp, a device that could de-materialize matter. He displayed actual laser beams, constructed a type of button lamp that could disintegrate any material, including zirconia and diamonds. The inventor handled enormous voltages through his body by increasing the frequency, or alterations per second, but with reduced amplitude. He would send tens of thousands of volts through and around his body, while holding two illuminated fluorescent tubes in each hand. He is credited with being the father of wireless.

On March 1, 1893, the Chicago World's Fair opened using the Tesla polyphase AC, a system that illuminated the entire fair and generated three times more energy than that used by the entire city of Chicago.

Competition was keen to harness Niagara Falls. Tesla's system, along with Westinghouse, was the only practical solution, building generators, switchers and auxiliary equipment necessary to do the task in 1899.

In 1898, Tesla designed a remote-controlled robotic boat and exhibited it at the Madison Square Garden. This single invention established all the essential principles for the development of radio, wireless-telephone, garage door openers, the car radio, facsimile machines, television, cable TV, scramblers, and remote-controlled robotics.

Tesla developed many other inventions. However, throughout his life, others tried to steal or take credit for his inventions. He died penniless in a New York hotel in January 1943. The Office of Alien Property seized all his papers, etc., and kept them for war security.

CHAPTER 93

Motivator/Teacher

Dale Carnegie

Dale Carnegie (1888-1955) was born in Harmony Church, Missouri. The family moved several times while Dale was growing up. The final move in 1904 put him in Warrensburg, Missouri, about three miles out of town. The family experienced years of poverty. Raising milk cows, beef cattle, and pigs, the Carnageys (original spelling) also raised wheat and corn. The rich farmland produced crops, but usually got flooded out by the river around harvest time.

Skinny Dale, with patched and tattered clothes, watched as the water drowned the crops. The family was so in debt that there was no money for new clothes. One year they had bumper crop, but so did every other farmer as prices plummeted. The Carnegies made a net profit of thirty dollars for one year's work.

Dale was a skinny, underfed, tow-headed boy, with big ears; he was the image of Tom Sawyer. One day he and friends were playing in a deserted building. As he jumped from the attic, his ring caught on a nail and tore off his forefinger. After that, with three fingers and a thumb, he felt self-conscious.

Amanda, Dale' mother, was a devout Methodist and wanted her sons to become missionaries, ministers, and schoolteachers. Her faith helped his father through discouraging years. Dale worried about death, lightning, and talking with girls. He was subjected to constant teasing about his big ears. One boy actually threatened to cut off his ears.

In 1904, Dale enrolled in Warrensburg State Teachers College. After chores, he would ride his horse three miles to school. Poor as he was, he discovered that he could stand up and speak with vitality and enthusiasm. Entering dozens of speaking contests, he lost them all. He saw himself as a social outcast, shunned by classmates.

He worked harder memorizing the words of Abraham Lincoln and others. A year later, Dale Carnegie won the school-wide speaking contest. In addition, he won the debating contest where he had previously been a social failure. He was now regarded as an intellectual leader. Other students came to him for training and advice.

In 1908, Carnegie left college and traveled to Denver and secured a sales job with International Correspondence Schools. Carnegie did not have success selling for the company and soon left to work for Armour and Company. Assigned to the Dakota Territory, he made $17.31 per week. By hard work, he rose to the number one position in the territory. Turning down a management position, he left for Newark City. There he was accepted into the American Academy of Dramatic Arts. The $400 fee took most of his savings. Upon graduation, Carnegie auditioned and was accepted for a part in *Pony of the Circus*.

After ten months of acting, Carnegie gave up and obtained a job selling Packard automobiles, but his real desire was to become a writer. Quitting his job, he started teaching public speaking at the YMCA. In the years following 1912, Carnegie refined and perfected his sessions. What Carnegie saw in his classes would eventually lead him to write *How to Stop Worrying and Start Living*. To earn a living, he asked for two dollars per session, settling for a profit-sharing basis, which had him earning $30 per night. He discovered he didn't have to sell a product to be a salesman. Selling his skills and ability, he achieved his original goal of having time to write. Dale Carnegie taught about overcoming fear, having positive reinforcement and self-confidence, and developing memory skills.

His book, *How to Win Friends and Influence People*, became one of the best-sellers of all time. A one-man program that began in a YMCA classroom in 1912 has grown to an international network of instructors. He has helped millions of people to achieve goals and better themselves.

CHAPTER 94

Activist/Service

Jane Addams

As a little girl, Jane Addams (1860-1935) was focused on service. She had a concern for those who were poor. "When I grow up, I want to build a beautiful house, then I will invite all the poor people to come and stay with me." Always asking questions, her father could see she had a strong desire to learn. He rewarded her by giving her 5 cents for every book she read and understood.

To help others, Addams figured she needed to be prepared, so she studied literature, math, science, and history. After graduating from Rockford Female Seminary in 1881, Addams sought a way to help the sick and destitute. Due to a bad back, she had to drop out of medical school.

Searching for new ideas, she traveled to London in 1888 and discovered Toynbee Hall. There, Oxford students taught classes and helped organize activities for the poor. Addams liked the idea and knew she could do the same in Chicago.

Addams, along with her friend Ellen Starr, went into one of the city's poorest areas and rented an old house built by Charles Hull, renting the second floor for $30 a month. With fresh paint and carpentry to make a welcoming interior, she talked wealthy friends into donating furniture. She invited all her neighbors over to see it. When working mothers complained that they had nowhere to leave their kids, Addams started a nursery and day care. She offered music and cooking lessons and organized games. At first, few people visited or attended her programs, but with constant urging, people came to see her. By the end of the year, Hull House had attracted more than 50,000 visitors.

One night in 1889, Addams was sleeping in Hull House and a burglar broke through a window and demanded money. Instead of panicking, she asked him why he needed the money. "I'm hungry and I can't find a job," he answered. Addams, remembering the principles of service on which she organized her house, said she would lend him money but on the condition that, "If you really want a job, come back tomorrow." The next day the would-be burglar returned and found himself a job. Before long, he had repaid Addams all the money.

Understanding that poverty knew no boundaries, she welcomed people of all races and religions. She even learned German, French and Italian so she could speak to people in their own language. When a wealthy landowner offered to donate buildings, she asked that the buildings be raised and the empty lot be given to her to build Chicago's first playground; this was in 1892. In 1894, Addams persuaded the mayor to build public bathhouses and to clean up the overflowing garbage by getting appointed garbage inspector.

For 40 years, Addams expanded Hull House to a full block, lobbied to pass a law forbidding children under 14 to work, promoted laws to protect women workers, and make factories cleaner and safer. Addams championed peace and voting rights for women. In 1931, she was awarded the Nobel Peace Prize for her work.

CHAPTER 95

Author/Cookbooks

Fannie Merrit Farmer

When Fannie Merrit Farmer (1857-1915) was in high school in Boston, she suffered a stroke. As a result, she quit high school. To earn a living, she went to work as a helper for a well-to-do family, the Shaws. Here she enjoyed cooking for the family and their friends. Complimented on her skills, they asked how they could duplicate some of the dishes they liked.

Farmer analyzed her cooking and started writing down how she made specific dishes, experimenting until she had precise measurements so that the dish could be made to taste, exactly the same again.

In the 1870s, recipes were passed down from mother to daughter, but they weren't written down. Farmer decided to put together a recipe book so the family favorites could be made over again, without guessing the ingredients. When she went to a restaurant, she would save a little sample and try to duplicate it at home.

Foreign travel wasn't affordable, so she would do the next best thing by going down to Boston Harbor to meet incoming ships to talk with foreigners and taste what they had to offer. Listening carefully to any tips, she would try to incorporate them into her own recipes.

Deciding to perfect her skills, she enrolled at Boston Cooking School. Farmer studied under Mary Lincoln, a well-known cook. After a few years studying, she helped edit the school's cookbook. Graduating in 1889, she later became an assistant director of the school. In 1894, she became its director.

Economic trends were up, and more families had more money to purchase new books. Also, more families could afford to hire help. Instead of performing chores like scrubbing and cleaning, the wife or mother now had more time for cooking and entertaining.

Farmer thought the time was ripe to do a new version of the *Boston Cooking School Cook Book*. Standardizing cooking measurements, she got rid of such measurements as "enough water to float an egg," or a "goblet full of wine." Precise terms reduced the chances of bad-tasting food.

She looked for a publisher, but publishers told her she was crazy to publish thousands of books that people didn't want. Farmer stuck to her plan, going from publisher to publisher, until she found one who would do the book her way. The book went on to become one of the world's best-selling recipe books, and it is still sold today.

In 1902, Farmer started Miss Farmer's School of Cookery. The purpose of the school was to cater to housewives, rather than professional chefs. She advised students to taste their dishes before serving them to others. She asked her students to always look for better ways to cook.

Farmer was never married and was a pioneer in her field. Her standards have earned her the title of "mother of level measurement."

CHAPTER 96

Composer/Ragtime

Scott Joplin

Scott Joplin (1868-1917) was born in Cave Springs, Texas. When he was young, he learned to play the banjo at age 7 and the piano at 11. He learned to play by ear, and his mother encouraged him. When his father left, his mother saved enough to buy Scott a second-hand piano. To get the money for sheet music and books, he carried water to railroad workers.

Later, Joplin took a job as a piano player on a Mississippi River steamboat. Realizing that he needed to develop his own style to stand apart, he went to St. Louis in 1888. Improvising with his notes, he distinguished himself from his ragtime peers. Before long, his style was so recognizable that people in the streets could identify his music.

In 1893, Joplin traveled to the World's Fair in Chicago, hoping to play some of his new ragtime music. He soon found out that his ragtime music wasn't welcomed within the fairgrounds. He was disappointed. How could he hope to get his music published when many audiences wouldn't even hear it?

Joplin wanted most of all to compose and publish his own works. To do so was a heavy task for a black man in his day. But Joplin had faith in his abilities. To better his skills, he enrolled in classes at Smith College of Music in Sedalia, Missouri. Arriving penniless, Joplin worked at a tavern and joined the Queen City Concert Band to pay his tuition. He also formed another band to play at parties and social functions to improve his skills.

Joplin realized he needed a steady job, so he took a job as a resident pianist at Sedalia's Maple Leaf Club. Working on his writing, he soon wrote his first two rags: "Original Rag" and "Maple Leaf Rag." Turned down by the first publisher, he knew that a song that was danceable would be a good seller. Approaching the next publisher, he brought along a boy who knew dancing, and the publisher was convinced to publish his song, "Maple Leaf Rag."

When his song hit the market in St. Louis in 1900, it sold 50,000 copies in the first few months. Between 1901 and 1903, Joplin published 16 new pieces. Joplin relied on a formula when writing. He began with a brief introduction followed by an upbeat melody, called the chorus, and then alternated between the two and concluding with a closing melody of the original key of the chorus.

In 1908, he wrote a ragtime opera called *Treemonisha*. After it played just one time in a theater in 1915, it was adjudged a failure. But long after his death, his opera hit Broadway in 1975 and was a success. In 1972, his songs were featured in the film *The Sting*, which won Oscars for best soundtrack, and title song, Joplin's "The Entertainer," renamed "The Sting."

CHAPTER 97

Entrepreneur/Dancing

Arthur Murray

Arthur Murray Teichman (1895-1991) was born in New York City. As a child, he was a bashful, awkward wallflower. It wasn't until he went to high school that he figured out how to dance, thanks to tutoring by a girlfriend.

Taking lessons, and always improving his steps, he practiced until he was dreaming up dance moves. It wasn't long until Murray was winning dance contests and teaching others to dance.

After high school, he secured a job at an architect's office drawing fine lines and planning buildings. He made it a point to learn as much about business and drafting as he could. At night, though, he kept his dreams alive by dancing. That's when Murray perfected his fox-trot, waltz and tango.

Murray believed if he could learn the fox-trot, anyone could. This idea became the core value of his business. At first he taught lessons only in the evenings. By 1912, he'd earned enough money to quit the architecture business and start his own dance school. His foremost rule on the dance floor was simple, "Know your steps!" That became his business philosophy.

In 1919, he enrolled at Georgia Institute of Technology to learn more about business. During his spare time, he tutored pupils in learning to dance at Atlanta's Georgian Terrace. He told pupils to visualize dance moves even when they were far away from the ballroom.

By 1920, he knew he wanted to teach the world to dance. To be able to teach thousands, he came up with the idea of giving dance instruction by mail. Murray, who dropped his last name in 1914, sent out large diagrams of dancing footprints featuring easy-to-follow lines and arrows. His architectural training had come in handy. People from all over the nation came to rely on Murray's renderings to master the dance steps.

Murray realized that, for many people, knowing how to dance spelled security in social situations. He was selling more than dancing, he was selling confidence. His advertisements read, "30 days ago they laughed at me," with a man surrounded by fawning women. It lured millions to take dancing lessons from Murray.

His company, Arthur Murray Inc., began franchising in 1938 and eventually came to include hundreds of dance studios. His advice to managers was to give each student undivided attention. In 1950, Murray bought 15 months of airtime on CBS-TV. He and his wife, Kathryn danced for the country. The show was a hit. Later he moved to ABC-TV where his *Arthur Murray Dance Party* was on the air for 10 years.

In 1964, Murray stepped down as president. At that time, the corporation was grossing more than $25 million annually.

CHAPTER 98

Inventor/Photography

Louis Jacques Daguerre

L ouis Jacques Daguerre (1787-1851) was born in
Cormeilles-en-Parisis, France. At the time, there was a
shortage of teachers following the revolution. There was little
opportunity for formal schooling. Although curious, he had few
books to study.

Louis showed an early talent in drawing, and he practiced art
eagerly. Apprenticing with a local architect, he sculpted designs
slowly, shaping his skills. At age 16, his heart lay in studying art.

His father disapproved because an artist's life held no financial
guarantee. So to find his true path, he left for Paris in 1804. Going
to work for a stage designer, Daguerre found a creative outlet for
painting panoramas for the theatre.

Melodrama relied heavily on excitement and spectacle. As the
visual aspect assumed more importance, word of Daguerre's dazzling
lighting and stage effects spread. Between 1816 and 1822, he
designed scenery for 13 melodramas at the Theatre Ambigu-
Comique, in Paris. His sets made him famous.

Constantly experimenting with new techniques, he and a
colleague developed a painting on a translucent screen to create
special effects in 1822. A daytime scene faded into night by

decreasing the light from the front and increasing the light from behind.

Daguerre used a dark chamber to record topographical views of his diagram and to make sketches for his stage designs. It was a small, lightproof box with a pinhole or lens on one side and a translucent screen on the other side where it captured an image in the lens and flashed it on the screen. An artist then traced the inverted image.

To speed up the process, he searched for a method of chemically fixing the image onto paper. In 1814, he learned of Joseph Nicephore Niepce's similar experiments that had invented heliography, a process by which crude images were produced on bitumen-coated pewter plates.

Through trial and error, he experimented with nitrite and chloride of silver, finally arriving upon plates of metal and glass for sensitive coatings. To make better progress, he teamed up with Niepce in 1829. For three years, he collaborated with Niepce, until he died in 1833.

Refusing to halt his research, Daguerre experimented with iodine on silver plates. Sensing the results with iodine, in 1831, he noticed the light sensitivity of silver iodine. By 1837, after hundreds of experiments, he found that he could fix an image by developing the silver iodine plate with mercury vapor, then rising it with a solution of common salt.

When he felt he had perfected the process, he announced his invention, in January 1839, to the Academy of Sciences. When the first daguerreotypes were displayed, people were entranced. They were well suited for the mass production of photographic portraits.

It was the "greatest discovery since that of the printing press," noted Sir Robert Robertson, president of the Royal Society in 1953.

CHAPTER 99

Entrepreneur/Prudential Insurance Company

John Fairfield Dryden

John F. Dryden (1839-1911) didn't invent life insurance, but he made it what we know today. Before him, it was a luxury for the rich. He made insurance available to everyone.

He suffered years of rejection and near failure of his insurance company before he reached his goal. Growing up poor, he worked any job he could find, saving enough to study at Yale. In school, he learned of the "private benevolent societies" of London. The groups offered "industrial insurance" to the working poor on a small weekly installment plan.

Studying every aspect of the insurance business, Dryden learned by selling insurance himself. Working night and day, he came upon a plan for his own company. In 1875, he founded the Prudential Friendly Society in New Jersey, with $30,000 from investors. His company offered life insurance of up to $500 for as little as 3 cents a week. Agents working on commission went into the neighborhoods to collect every week. Knowing people trusted neighbors more than strangers, he hired neighborhood women as agents. Before long, the company's business grew. It had a reputation for paying out claims within 24 hours. Letters from grateful customers were used as advertisements. However, something was wrong. After 2 years, the company was still in the red. By

1876, it had sold 7,000 policies and had a deficit of $1,500. The investors grew nervous.

Dryden decided he needed a new approach. Going to England, he re-examined insurance companies there to find out what he was doing wrong. He realized from the study that his actuarial tables were off. He hadn't taken into account the dangerous jobs that many of the policyholders held. He also discovered that premium rates were too low. Third, he had offered sickness insurance, something British companies found unprofitable. He also realized that selling just in New Jersey did not give the company a large enough base of customers.

Mistakes are just learning experiences, Dryden thought. Taking full responsibility for his errors, he was brutally honest in his assessments and regained the confidence of his investors.

He opened up offices in Pennsylvania and New York after revising the business model. By 1885, Prudential Insurance Company had assets of $1 million. Having been successful in business, Dryden wanted to help his country. In 1902, he won a special election to the U.S. Senate. While there, he was a key sponsor of a seemingly impossible project, the Panama Canal. At the end of his term, he stepped down for health reasons. He died four years later in 1911. His personal fortune was then $50 million.

"To have had faith in a new idea is not rare, for the world is full of dreamers who hopelessly struggle against overwhelming odds. But to have an abiding faith in an almost hopeless aim and effort and to have carried the idea through the years, against all odds to a successful termination, is given to few men like John F. Dryden. A truly great man of his time," said his hometown newspaper, the *Newark Expositor*, in 1909.

CHAPTER 100

Determination/Flying Tigers

Lt. Gen. Claire Lee Chennault

Claire Lee Chennault (1893-1958) was born in Commerce, Texas. As a youth, he learned to overcome obstacles. When he was 16 years old, he enrolled in the Reserve Officer Training Corps at Louisiana State University. The regular army officer in charge told him he would never make a soldier.

Chennault didn't give up; he buckled down, graduated and went after his goal from another angle, by teaching elementary and high school at a one-room schoolhouse in Athens, Georgia. The pupils in high school were unruly, so few teachers lasted more than a term. Chennault invited the biggest, overgrown farm boys to go out behind the schoolhouse with him. Here, he fought them with bare knuckles, one by one, and beat them all. Instead of resenting Chennault, the boys became his ardent champions, and discipline was achieved.

But his thoughts were on becoming a soldier. He also discovered flying the first time he saw an airplane. He signed up in 1917 for flight school. He was rejected for not possessing the qualifications to becoming an aviator. Taking another track, he applied for the Infantry. Before long, his leadership skills earned him the rank of first lieutenant in the 90th Infantry Division.

To make sure he still wanted to fly, he talked an officer at Kelly Field into giving him a ride in a Jenny. That fueled his desire to fly. Determined to make his dream a reality, he learned everything he could about airplane mechanics, until his superiors let him go to the flight school. In 1919, he became one of the army's best pursuit pilots.

By 1937, Captain Chennault was forced out of the Army Air Corps because of bad hearing and chronic bronchitis. Also, pilots of the day preached that no fighter plane could take down a bomber. Bombers flew higher than fighters, they said. Chennault argued that with teamwork and strategy they could win against bombers. These views didn't win a lot of friends and it was rumored, which is why he was forced out of the Army Air Corps.

Chennault was not about to sit back, so he took a job in Kumming, China, as an advisor to the China Aeronautical Commission, he whipped its Air Force into shape. In 1941, he was convinced that the Japanese were a real threat and he talked President Roosevelt and his staff into sending a covert force to defend China from the Japanese. During the summer, 112 volunteer pilots arrived at Toungoo, China, to get his American volunteer group in shape, He started the day at 6 A.M. with push-ups followed by hours of flight training. When it was too hot to fly, he schooled them in the ways of war.

His first lesson: Work together, because in combat you're a team. Two planes fighting together were more effective than four planes fighting alone. Lesson two: Know your enemy like the back of your hand. Using captured Japanese flying manuals, he instructed them in the enemy's tactics. Study them, and you will always be one step ahead of the enemy.

Lesson three: Do the unexpected, break up their formations. Fourth: Focus, make every bullet count. To encourage teamwork, his men played baseball in their free time. Chennault upped morale by getting his men to paint the fronts of their planes with the savage gaze of tiger sharks.

By December 1941, the Flying Tigers were like a sharpened spear. They provided protection for the Burma Road, a crucial supply route between Rangoon and Chongqing. During the seven months after, the Japanese attack on Pearl Harbor, the Flying Tigers shot down 296 Japanese planes. For a time, the Flying Tigers provided the only victories in the Far East.

By 1942, his China Air Task Force was defending the air supply route over the Himalayan Mountains. Chennault was awarded the rank of lieutenant general in the same year. After the end of World War II, he organized Flying Tiger Airlines.

CHAPTER 101

Integrity/Forrester

Frederick Weyerhaeuser

Born in Niedersaulheim, Germany, Frederick Weyerhaeuser (1834-1914) was the only surviving son of a farmer. When his father died young, Frederick, age 12, quit school to run the family's 15-acre farm and 3-acre vineyard. Doing well enough to pay expenses, they had something left over, but other family members who'd emigrated to America sent back "encouraging" reports about the U.S.

In 1852, the family decided to follow and settled in Pennsylvania where Frederick went to work in a brewery. He doubled his salary (from $4 a month to $9) in one year. His plan was to make brewing his life, but gave it up when he saw how often brewers became drunkards.

Moving to Illinois in 1856, he found work in a saw mill. Soon he was promoted to a manager in a branch lumberyard. Things went well until a poor deal forced the company out of business. Learning his trade well, his resourcefulness attracted the attention of one of the creditors. He suggested Weyerhaeuser buy the lumber assets and even offered to finance the purchase.

During this time, there was economic panic, but he took up the offer and through good management, Weyerhaeuser had to be very flexible to make ends meet. He traded lumber for horses, oxen, hogs, and eggs from farmers who needed barns and houses. These he traded for logs from the rafts on the banks of the Mississippi River and repeated the process until he had cleared $8,000.

In 1860, he and his brother-in-law purchased the Rock Island Mill and formed Weyerhaeuser and Denkman. This became the foundation of Weyerhaeuser, Inc. He was the first operator to understand that to survive large quantities of trees were needed.

Realizing that people would always need lumber, he began to invest in timber, which became a lifelong habit. When a friend criticized him for purchasing timber at a high price, Weyerhaeuser replied, "I know this much. Whenever I buy, I make a profit. Whenever I do not buy, I miss an opportunity." In 1900, he purchased hundreds of thousands of acres of prime forest in the Pacific Northwest. Dozens laughed at him, but he was very optimistic. He looked to the future because his concern was that the country would run out of timber. "This (purchase) is not for us nor our children, but it is for our grandchildren."

Weyerhaeuser was also known for his ability to innovate. For years, loggers branded their logs and threw them in the river, and when they reached the mill—with others—they would try to find their logs. Weyerhaeuser said it would be a good idea to grade the logs first so they could take out an equivalent of what they had put in the river instead of hunting for their own logs.

Today Weyerhaeuser sells more lumber than any other company in the world. Weyerhaeuser did well. His secret lay simply in readiness to work. He never counted the hours or knocked off until he finished what he had in hand.

(POSTSCRIPT)

Here listed are 101 ways that you can develop, discover, and learn of the talents that may be dormant inside you. These 101 ways can make you a better person, and may even make you rich both in mind and circumstances.

1) Find a cure for Alzheimer's Disease.
2) Develop a better zipper.
3) Discover a way to prevent wheels on vehicles from appearing to be spinning backwards in movies.
4) Learn a foreign language.
5) Develop a better way to predict the weather.
6) Discover a cure for Parkinson's Disease.
7) Invent a better lightbulb.
8) Invent a more efficient automotive engine.
9) Prove that perpetual motion will work.
10) Find a better way to make closure on clothes than buttons.
11) A way to lessen sonic booms from fast flying planes.
12) Find a cure for Sickle Cell Anemia
13) A lawnmower that cuts grass, mulches, and compacts into a small amount of space and could possibly recycle into something useful.
14) Develop a better, or different, microwave stove for cooking foods.
15) Invent socks that don't develop holes.
16) A way to get instant hot or cold water out of our tap without running the water and wasting it down the drain.

17) A better road material than asphalt or concrete that resists cracks as a result of expansion and contraction due to weather.

18) A way to genetically kill flies and mosquitoes.

19) Learn to play a musical instrument, such as a piano, guitar, etc.

20) Learn to read music.

21) Take singing lessons.

22) Learn pottery making.

23) Take watercolor painting lessons.

24) Learn to dance.

25) Find a cure for a specific type of cancer.

26) Find a way to keep dogs from barking incessantly at everything.

27) Write a book or article of interest to you and others and publish it.

28) Learn to paint in oils.

29) Develop a thread or sewing system that prevents clothes from falling apart.

30) An automobile that never drips oil from the motor and transmission.

31) A way to prevent tooth decay in the water system, other than fluoride, that is safe.

32) A regular envelope that does not require wetting.

33) A traffic stop sign that beeps at you if you don't come to a full stop behind that line.

34) A way to discourage people from driving over the speed limit other than radar.

35) A better way to repair cuts in the road that are made for utility repairs and installation.

36) A more efficient way to dry clothes than in the present clothes dryer.

37) A cheaper replacement for newsprint in printing newspapers, magazines, etc.

38) Find a cure for, or to prevent, leukemia.

39) A better way to remove water and snow from auto and truck windshields.

40) A way to kill bugs and spiders in your house without the use of poisons.
41) Solve the problem of bad breath.
42) A plan, or a way, to cut down on the number of divorces.
43) A way to prevent wars from starting that is a win-win situation for both sides.
44) Wireless locks for file cabinets.
45) A way to prevent lightning from interfering with AM radio reception.
46) Learn to repair watches
47) Learn how to make decorative pins for wearing.
48) Write short stories that inspire youth and adults.
49) Develop a showerhead and faucet that saves water.
50) Plant a garden and raise your own vegetables and fruits.
51) Trace your ancestry back as far as you can go and publish a history of your ancestors.
52) Take a public speaking course to increase your skills.
53) Find a cure or a way to prevent diabetes type one and two.
54) Discover a method to keep sidewalks and driveways from cracking.
55) Join a service club in your community and give back to others.
56) Paint your own house or apartment. Study how to be good at it.
57) Learn how to do carpentry and make or build things.
58) Learn to crochet or knit an item.
59) Learn how to do floral arrangements.
60) Find a cure for Acquired Immune Deficiency Syndrome (AIDS)
61) Develop a plan for the elimination of malaria.
62) Learn mountain climbing and make some plans to scale one.
63) Invent an economic way to convert hydrogen from water and apply it to powering engines.
64) Invent a train whistle that can only be heard in immediate danger area.
65) Develop or learn to make a budget for your home or business.

66) Invent a way to keep lint from sticking to clothes.
67) Follow a consistent diet and exercise program.
68) Adopt a philosophy of only saying good things about other people.
69) Learn how to do you own plumbing.
70) Conceive and draw a new comic strip.
71) Develop an automobile tire that will last 100,000 miles with proper maintenance.
72) Solve the problem of gophers in a lawn or field without the use of poison or shooting them.
73) Coin a new word that becomes accepted into the dictionary.
74) Develop a carpet that resists getting dirty.
75) Invent a cereal that is healthy with no sugar that both children and adults crave.
76) A way to interest people in studying the Scriptures.
77) A health plan that allows people to live to 120 years or more without a major illness.
78) A retirement home that both the healthy and the ill can live in that brings out the best in people.
79) Invent a way to overcome weather inversions in valley areas.
80) A way to turn fall leaves into a useful product besides mulch.
81) A way to discourage drivers from "tailgating."
82) A decorative fire hydrant made in the form of an animal or person.
83) Discover or invent a way to eliminate fog at airports without using dry ice particles dropped from the air.
84) A way to discourage people from becoming anorexic.
85) A commercial use for tumbleweeds.
86) Become an optimist by always looking at the positive side of things.
87) Take up the hobby of bird watching—join the Audubon Society.
88) Learn to write poetry.
89) Learn to tie fishing flies.
90) Volunteer as a candy striper at your local hospital.

91) Take up photography. Learn to develop your own prints.

92) Learn how to work on automobile engines by taking a training course at local community college.

93) Learn to shoot a shotgun and take up the sport of shooting "clay pigeons."

94) Take a professional sales training course and get into a vocation where good salespeople are always in demand.

95) Take professional golf lessons—you could become the next Tiger Woods.

96) Take up the sport of archery.

97) Discover a way to lessen the impact of hurricanes and tornadoes.

98) Develop a mailbox that prevents theft.

99) Invent automobile brakes that last twice as long.

100) Write the words and music to a song and have it published.

101) Develop the ability to remember names of people, places and things. Improve your outlook on life by taking a self-improvement class such as Dale Carnegie's course.

BVG